DARE TO CONNECT

DARE TO CONNECT

Redefining Success for the Modern Educator

Belle O'Neill

ROWMAN & LITTLEFIELD
Lanham • Boulder • New York • London

Published by Rowman & Littlefield
An imprint of The Rowman & Littlefield Publishing Group, Inc.
4501 Forbes Boulevard, Suite 200, Lanham, Maryland 20706
www.rowman.com

6 Tinworth Street, London SE11 5AL, United Kingdom

Copyright © 2021 by Belle O'Neill

All rights reserved. No part of this book may be reproduced in any form or by any electronic or mechanical means, including information storage and retrieval systems, without written permission from the publisher, except by a reviewer who may quote passages in a review.

British Library Cataloguing in Publication Information Available

Library of Congress Cataloging-in-Publication Data Available

ISBN 9781475862683 (cloth : alk. paper) | ISBN 9781475862690 (pbk. : alk. paper) | ISBN 9781475862706 (epub)

∞ ™ The paper used in this publication meets the minimum requirements of American National Standard for Information Sciences Permanence of Paper for Printed Library Materials, ANSI/NISO Z39.48-1992.

To the faculty, staff, and students at
McQueen High School, Reno, Nevada,
and to my husband, Mike,
and our children, Liane and John

CONTENTS

Foreword ix
Preface xi
Acknowledgments xiii
Introduction xv

PART I: CREATING SUCCESS AT SCHOOL   1

1. Present and Joyful Connections   3
2. Prepared with Calm Transitions   7
3. Part of the Team: Benefits   41
4. Positive Investments Make a Meaningful Career   45
5. Proactive Leader: Creating a Positive Classroom Climate   51
6. Patience and Humor in the Classroom   71

PART II: CREATING SUCCESS OUTSIDE OF THE CLASSROOM   75

7. Present for You First and Then for Others   77
8. Prepared and Not Frazzled   81
9. Part of the Team: Knowing Your Colleagues Outside of School   83
10. Positive: An Identity Outside of School   85
11. Proactive Leader: Standing Up for Your Teacher Rights   87
12. Patient: Growing from Experiences   105

PART III: CREATING SUCCESS AFTER RETIRING FROM TEACHING — 109

13 Be Present to the End of Your Career and Retire on Your Terms — 111

14 Prepare Financially and Emotionally for Retirement — 115

15 Part of a New Team and New Interests — 119

16 Positive: Retirement Is an Attitude and Not an Event — 121

17 Proactive Leader: Create What You Want to Happen in Retirement — 123

18 Patient in Your Transition to Retirement — 125

Conclusion: Leading Changes from the Classroom — 127

Bibliography — 145

Index — 151

About the Author — 155

FOREWORD

"You are the author of your life script now."

In *Dare to Connect: Redefining Success for the Modern Educator*, Belle O'Neill has zoned in on an essential element that a teacher often forgets about in their career: own it. Though teachers "command" their classroom and "give out" grades, the fact of the matter is they are subject to the demands and opinions of others, so they can easily lose sight of the fact that they are indeed experts. Based on the author's long career as a public-school teacher, this book offers advice for developing and deepening expertise for teachers at every career stage.

New teachers will find this book an excellent source for practical and pragmatic advice. As a teacher educator, I know new teachers are worried about many of the areas the author addresses—from structuring classroom procedures, giving homework, and handling cell phones, to establishing a classroom presence, understanding parents, and working with colleagues.

Mid-level teachers can find information to expand their horizons and interests, which may help them find more ways to enjoy and be involved in their work. Most notable here is the author's discussion of global competence. In a century defined by globalism, it is disheartening to see how often it is overlooked in teaching. The COVID pandemic of 2020 has made painfully clear that global understanding and skills are not just nice additional skills anymore; they are necessary and urgent.

If teachers do not pursue knowledge about the world and model and emphasize global competence skills to their students, who will? The author's strong emphasis in this area is a hallmark of this book. It is incredibly valuable information not often found in books addressed at teachers across all grades and content areas.

For the experienced teacher, the section on teacher leadership may help teachers gain confidence and see how much their perspective and experience can change the teaching and learning experience. All teachers are on the front lines and can be the strongest advocates for change, but it can be easy to get into a rut and stay there. The author has explained a variety of ways the expert teacher can become a leader.

Finally, expert teachers might find it refreshing to read about preparing for and living beyond retirement. So many "teachers" books are only aimed at those in a classroom, but the author describes ways not only to manage the transition but to make the most of it.

We know that one of the essential skills of a great teacher is being a lifelong learner. All teachers, going into or having exited from the classroom, will find something of interest in this book that can help them develop and continue in their role as learning experts.

—Jennifer Mahon, PhD
Associate Professor, Secondary Education
University of Nevada, Reno
Fellow, International Academy of Intercultural Research

PREFACE

We live in a society where educational stakeholders—teachers, students, parents, administrators, and the community—are out of touch with each other. Parents can no longer help in classrooms due to safety concerns. Teachers have no time to collaborate with colleagues during the school day. Students and teachers clash over cell phones versus creating a real classroom community.

Administrators use e-mails to convey their directives to teachers. School boards make decisions independently of teachers, administrators, and the public. Universities prepare students for teaching careers in content and methodology, but more emphasis is needed on building relationships among stakeholders.

This book prepares teachers for what is ahead: what to expect when they are teaching. It is a guide for how to navigate between the stakeholders to become the successful educator. Successful educators take the time to establish connections with their stakeholders because that establishes them as a professional teacher: someone these groups can trust and work with.

This is how to enjoy a fulfilling teaching career and avoid struggles with these groups resulting in burnout. This is how to communicate and set boundaries with the above stakeholders so they can work together as equals, solve problems together, and improve student learning.

This book is for teachers at all points in their careers: the new teacher eager to make a difference but looking for guidance on how, when, and why it is so important to lead professionally without burning themselves out in the process; the midway teacher needing motivation and the courage to make changes so they are not on automatic pilot and their career is more meaningful for them and their students; and the teacher at the end of their career needing help on closure, how to transition gracefully into retirement, and how to still contribute to society.

No matter where you are in your career, this book will give you new ideas or validate what you already know and why.

You are a member of a teaching profession, but you must consistently display professionalism to be treated like one. I define professionalism with my six criteria, the six Ps, based on my thirty-two years' experience as a classroom teacher. These six criteria may be used as a checklist to establish connections and build your reputation throughout your career. Use these as a reference when you have issues. Use these to give you confidence when you must speak up for yourself.

It is important to be professional because, first, it is easier and less stressful. Second, you will be taken more seriously and respected. Third, you will avoid burnout. Fourth, all other professions and vocations are possible because they had professional teachers. Fifth, you cannot collaborate with anyone else until you are confident in who you are. You must believe in yourself and feel you have something to offer. It is like a marriage: two equal halves coming together to share ideas and coming up with solutions.

Failing to act professionally sets a bad example and may cause you to lose trust in yourself, as well as students, colleagues, parents, the administration, and the community losing trust in you. There is a fine line between a caring adult and a friend. Safety and learning are the first priorities in a classroom. You represent your profession every day when you stand in front of your classroom. Be professional!

The six Ps do not include popular nor perfect. Your goal is to be respected by others and yourself and not to bend to each person's wishes so they like you. That is exhausting and unethical. Your job is to help students learn and not to win their approval. Another goal is to grow. You will make mistakes along the way and improve your teaching as a result. If you see perfection as the goal, you will be paralyzed because you will make unattainable goals or you will falsely believe once you have it all figured out, you can coast for the rest of your career. You do not get to coast for the rest of your career.

ACKNOWLEDGMENTS

Thank you to Dr. Jennifer Mahon for writing the foreword for this book. I am forever grateful for the opportunity to spend time with your university students and international teachers.

Thank you to teachers Peggy Hickman, Chris Case, Caroline Hatcher, Dan Gallaher, and Kathleen Whatford for reviewing this book and giving me valuable feedback.

Thank you to Jedda Phillips and Cathy Roth for inspiring me to go forward and never give up.

Thank you to Rowman & Littlefield for publishing this book and your team of editors for their patient guidance.

Thank you to the faculty, staff, and students at Swope Middle School in Reno, Nevada, where I first became a Spanish teacher. Former principal Bill Campbell, you made this possible.

Thank you to the faculty, staff, and students at McQueen High School in Reno, Nevada, for welcoming, encouraging, and supporting me in my growth as a teacher. I will always proudly be a Lancer.

Thank you to my brother and author Paul Gold, who taught me how to retire gracefully.

Thank you to my family: my husband, Mike, a retired teacher, who generously helped with technical support and reviewing this book multiple times. Thank you to my daughter, Liane, a professional communications specialist, who had great public relations advice for me. Thank you to my son, John, a future teacher, who spent many hours in my classroom helping me out.

INTRODUCTION

This book addresses the whole teacher from a humanistic perspective and is organized into three parts: the teacher at school, the teacher outside of the classroom, and the teacher in retirement. Each of these parts is further subdivided by the six criteria (the six Ps) of the professional teacher: present, prepared, part of the team, positive, proactive, and patient.

Through all three of these units is the recurring theme of connectedness: what the teacher creates at school affects what the teacher creates outside of school and vice versa. What the teacher created at school and outside of school affects what the teacher creates in retirement.

The final part of the book addresses the future of education: leading changes from the classroom with teachers as respected professional leaders and collaborators with their stakeholders.

Part I

Creating Success at School

Being professional at school means:

1. Present
2. Prepared
3. Part of the team
4. Positive
5. Proactive leader
6. Patient

I

PRESENT AND JOYFUL CONNECTIONS

The most important quality for a teacher is being present. This supersedes everything. When you are in the moment, you experience the joy and connection of teaching. You observe the process of learning when students work together on a project. You see the smile and eyes of a student who suddenly gets it. You acquire all the good stuff that keeps you going every day.

If a teacher is not present, they are not connecting and engaging with their students. They are not in tune with the current classroom environment, which affects how students learn that day. Be especially present when you teach the same lesson plan several times in a row. Every class is different and cannot be taught the same way.

From the moment the students arrive to when they leave the classroom, be there in the moment. Be at the door for every new student entering class. Greet them by name at the door, smile, and look them in the eye. A big smile and asking how they are doing goes a long way. It shows you care about them as a person and not only as a student in your class.

Be at the door for every new entering class. It is a great reset for you too because it gives you a break, a time to clear the slate. It sets a positive and welcoming tone for the classroom. It is a great time to individually talk with students about missing assignments, behavioral issues, dress code violations, or issues in their lives that are preventing them from fully participating in class that day. Talking with a student individually at the door is much more effective than talking with a student in front of the class where it could become a tug of war between you and the class.

You are creating a classroom community with the goals of learning and working together. Do not let any distractions like cell phones destroy this connection. Therefore, use this time at the door to remind students to put away their cell phones and ear buds in their backpacks before they enter, and cell phones are not to be seen nor heard until the students are beyond the classroom door. The door is the dividing line. That means no recharging the cell phones in the outlets around your classroom because then they are seen. It is the students' responsibility to recharge them at home and not your responsibility.

Have consequences written into your syllabus for cell phones seen or heard during classroom time. For example, the first time (there are no warnings) the cell phone is seen or heard, the student has to give it to the teacher and pick it up at the end of the day from the teacher.

Of course, students will test cell phone rules. If they return to you earlier in the day and say they have a doctor's appointment and need their cell phone, ask them to show you the excused early dismissal slip from the office. At that point, they will probably turn and walk away. Or, if they need it next period for a different class, have their next teacher call you on the phone and explain that to you. Chances are you will never hear from the next teacher.

The next time the cell phone is seen or heard and from there on, the phones are sent to the student relations office and the student has school-wide consequences. You need your school to be fully on board for this. If it is not, speak with your administration, and if they will not agree to school-wide consequences, see if they will approve your individual consequences in your syllabus.

Be wary of using cell caddies in the classroom. Not only do you give up class time picking up and redistributing them after class, but you are also responsible if any student steals them out of the cell caddy or refuses to turn one in. Instead, walk the room constantly and stand behind the class when they are working alone or in groups, so they know to be on task.

Cell phones are only allowed out if you are using them as a class and you give them permission to take them out. Tell the students when to put them away. You want your students present and not distracted with texting, reading e-mails, or taking photos of classmates, their teachers, or answer keys.

The first day of school before you take roll, announce that if you mispronounce a student's name, you need their help, and you need them to pronounce their name correctly. Take notes on a seating chart and write their names phonetically to help you remember. Ask them if they go by a different first name, for example their middle name, and honor that. As far as nicknames, that is up to you. If you do not feel comfortable calling them "Shorty," for example, take them aside and say you would prefer to call them by their given name. Pronouncing a student's name correctly says you care about them.

When you teach, put yourself in the students' shoes. Watch them carefully for verbal as well as nonverbal cues that they understand the concepts. Stop, back up, and reteach the lesson in a different way, if the students are lost. If you went into a doctor's office and they were on autopilot and not listening to you, imagine how you would feel. That is how a student feels when they are unheard and perhaps misdiagnosed.

Move around your classroom. Do not stay in the front of the room. You will be amazed how much is going on in the classroom related and not related to learning. It is like the cop waiting on the side of the road and suddenly everyone slows down and watches the speed limit. Students are held accountable when they see you wandering the classroom. Again, it shows you care that they are learning in your classroom. Most importantly, when you roam the classroom, you are more connected to the students as individuals.

Teaching is about relationships with your students. Insist on clear aisles and backpacks and other supplies underneath the desk. You must be able to get to every desk. The students must be able to exit quickly in an emergency evacuation without stumbling over backpacks. Announce to the students beforehand when you are there to help and when you are not there to help but only to observe their progress.

Start your class on time. State in your syllabus that students must be in their seats with all required supplies before the bell rings or they are tardy. Immediately have a daily review sponge, so you can catch your breath and take roll, while they settle down for class. Students like routine. Routines become habits. If you are consistent, your students will be consistent. This will also show the students that your class runs from bell to bell and that education is the priority in your classroom.

Have homework due at the beginning of class and plan for it to be passed forward immediately when the bell rings. Late homework is only accepted due to an excused absence or an excused tardy. Do not issue passes for students to return to their lockers for forgotten materials or assignments once the bell rings. You do not want them missing out on valuable class time. Quickly grade the homework—sometimes just for completion, sometimes accuracy in certain sections—and immediately go over it.

While you grade the homework, the students have an alternate individual writing activity related to the content currently being learned in class. Set a timer and announce how many minutes in which they must complete this classwork. As soon as the timer goes off, call on students randomly. Hold students accountable for their learning.

Place a transparency sheet over your seating chart. If you have a behavioral issue, note it with a dry erase marker on your seating chart and later put it in your record book by date, using an abbreviation like T for tardy. After entering all class notations, erase them at the end of each day.

The bell does not dismiss the students—you do! Dismiss them row by row after all garbage has been picked up off the floors and everything is out of the baskets beneath the desks. If you dismiss by rows, you will not have vandalism or bullying issues because you can watch the individual students. Also, if you dismiss the students, you will not have to do deal with students deciding to get out of their seats to edge toward the door before the bell rings and miss out on the final minutes of instruction.

Tell them they are not allowed to pack up until you tell them it is time. Again, this keeps students on task, and they are not in charge of when the instruction ends.

2

PREPARED WITH CALM TRANSITIONS

Be prepared just like a scout! Carry three umbrellas—one for the car, one for the classroom, and one for home. You never know when a downpour will catch you! Always overplan. Tight lesson plans prevent behavioral issues because the students do not have time to misbehave.

Be knowledgeable in your subject area. Be up on the latest information. Leadership of a classroom is important, but knowledge of your subject area also is. When you know your subject matter, you have more tools in your box. You can anticipate where students will struggle and preview this before you begin the lesson. You can teach your subject in logical, sequential, and manageable chunks for the students. You can reteach a concept in multiple ways if students do not understand the original presentation. You can answer students' questions beyond what you presented that day. You establish credibility with your students.

When you know your subject matter and are passionate about it, it comes across to your students. Your excitement fuels them. In fact, what motivates students is the usefulness of the information and its potential for impacting others. Therefore, teachers do need to demonstrate the relevance and the significance of their subject matter. Teachers do this by showing students the content's real-world connections and by involving students in activities that inspire creative applications.

For example, if your subject matter is Spanish, you could organize a two-week cultural exchange at your high school. Invite a small group of teachers and students from Colombia. Partner each guest student with a student from one of your Spanish classes. The Colombians follow the class schedule of their partner and attend all their classes daily, including your Spanish class.

The Colombians will stay at your students' homes. Send home a letter asking for interested parents to sign and return the letter. Choose the homes and set up a meeting with the parents and their children to discuss their responsibilities such as providing daily transportation to and from the school and three meals a day for the guests. Provide an information sheet on each guest to the home they will be staying at, including their allergies and interests. Have parents share any concerns they may have at this time. Mention parents can take their guests on family activities such as ice skating or visiting nearby towns.

You can coordinate group activities with community resources like your local university or television news station. Take your guests with bus transportation from the university to iconic locations like Lake Tahoe. Participate in events they do not have in their country due to climate or geography, for example, sledding in the snow. Have your news station run a story on the cultural exchange to promote global education.

The Colombians could host assemblies for your high school and dance their native dances. Your high school could put up large banners welcoming them to the school and interview them in the school newspaper.

Learning Spanish now has relevance. Students can now communicate with their new friends and learn about a new culture. The Colombian cultural exchange benefits not only your Spanish classes but also benefits the entire school as they see the dances of Colombia. Students now want to learn more about Colombia and perhaps visit it in the future.

Teachers can be relevant and apply their subject matter in less time-consuming ways. For example, invite a guest speaker to your classroom in your subject area. Instead of just having the speaker arrive, speak, answer questions, and leave, make this a more interactive learning experience.

Define your students' roles in learning from the guest speaker. Before the speaker's visit, have students learn more about the topic. Have each student prepare a list of questions, share those questions in small groups, and select a set of them to be asked by a student-selected panel. After the presentation, have the panel interview the speaker. All students need to take notes during the presentation and during the panel discussion.

After the speaker leaves or before the next class, have students reflect upon the guest speaker's presentation and connect this to the class objectives, the students' past experiences related to the topic, and upcoming course topics.

Authentic tasks require authentic assessments. For example, in the guest speaker experience, have students summarize the most important point of the guest speaker in one sentence. Then write why that was. Have students indicate if any of their questions to the presenter were not answered. Have students write three more questions they now have based on the presentation.

Plan outlines of large units the previous summer. Have your foundation set so you can fill in the details and have the resources needed before school begins in the fall.

Have necessary handouts printed at least one week ahead. Do not expect the department assistant, if you have one, to do your copying at the last minute. The department assistant could even copy your first month of school the previous May or June. What a great start of the year for you!

Write lesson plans once a week for the following week. Do not write them day by day. That is like grocery shopping every day instead of once a week. The goal here is efficiency and continuity. If you finish a lesson early, you can continue to the next day because you know what is ahead. Save your lesson plans in a hard-copy lesson planner or on your computer from year to year. You may not do the exact same thing, but why reinvent the wheel? Many lessons may be repeated the following year.

Teaching is like following a recipe. Go through the daily lesson(s) before school each day. Put key points on the board or project them on the screen. Make sure your technology is set up and ready to go. Pretend you are the student. Are your directions clear? Make sure all the ingredients (supplies) are ready and you have all the steps in place before you start the class. Run the lesson in your head before class. Where could there be confusion? How can you prevent this from happening?

Put handouts on the same daily designated table for the students to pick up before class. Teach them this from day one. Have a special area in your classroom where absent students can read from a binder what happened in class, pick up handouts, deposit homework, and pick up graded homework. This gives the students responsibility and ownership of their learning and education. It is not your job to stop class and catch them up. If they are still lost, they need to see you during your office hours. Include your weekly assignments in the binder as well as posting them online, so the students never have the excuse that they did not have access to a computer.

Reflection is a powerful tool where you look at what you do in your classroom and think about why you do it. Self-reflection never stops, especially when you are a veteran teacher. There is always something new to learn that will not only make you a better teacher but also improve student learning. It is tempting to skip this step with so many other things to do, but if you do not write down your thoughts, you may forget them and make the same mistakes the next time you teach the lesson. Also, you may learn new things about yourself and your students that you might not have noticed if you did not take the time to reflect.

Reflection can be natural but should also be planned and purposeful. To get a clear view about the state of your teaching, you need to gather information first.

1. Use exit slips to quickly gauge student understanding at the end of a lesson. You could ask questions like: Did you understand today's lesson? If not, what can the teacher do to improve your understanding? The answers will let you know if you need to back up and review information or if you can move ahead the next day (Renard 2019).
2. Include reflection in your lesson plan. Add a blank reflection section at the bottom of each of your lesson plans. After each lesson, look it over to see what you can improve the next time you teach it. Sometimes the written reflection applies to the specific lesson, but sometimes it applies to teaching in general. For example, you may write down you need to provide examples in each section of the homework that day before you assign it. Or you may write down you need to find a system to call on every student in the class each day, to make sure everyone understands the concepts and thus everyone is learning.
3. Utilize peer observations and reflections. Reflection is great alone but can be more powerful when done with others. Have an observer write clarifying and probing questions based on their observations of a lesson. After the class, the observer and the one being observed sit down and discuss the questions without unsolicited advice or judgment.

It is helpful to see the class from another person's viewpoint and to talk about details the person teaching the class may not have noticed; for example, note how they lead discussions, who they call on, how they move about the class, and the flow of the class. These reflections can bond the department because the teachers learn to trust each other.

1. Seek out student input. Gather students' opinions of your lessons to get a feel of them from their perspective. Do it informally by talking with small groups of students who stay late for help or discuss it with the entire class at the end of a unit or project. Do it formally by creating student surveys. Use surveys especially when you try something new but also at the middle and end of the school year as a general look back. You could use paper and pencil feedback forms but also go digital with the use of Google Forms.

No matter what the format, student input improves teaching because it is not what the teacher teaches as much as what the students learn. To reflect as a teacher is not just looking back at yourself in a mirror but looking back at yourself from the eyes of your students (Paul 2016).

1. Videotape your teaching. You can reflect not only on your teaching but also on your body language and classroom management. What did you learn about student learning and your teaching as you watched it? Did the video catch anything you did not notice while you were teaching? Videotaping can take some getting used to because you must make sure your students feel comfortable with a video camera in the room.

Also, make sure you follow the school district policy. Some districts require a permission form to be signed by the parents to videotape students. Other districts do not allow students' faces on screen, so the camera would need to be focused on the teacher and show only the backs of the students. That may involve altering usual classroom seating arrangements.

1. Use a reflective journal. Keep a notebook nearby so you can jot down comments and observations before, during, or after the lesson about what worked well, what did not, and why.

2. If you prefer not to write, quickly record one-minute reflections on your smart phone using the voice-recording app after each lesson. Do label the recordings so you can review the information again in the future.
3. Create a teacher mood board at the beginning of your teaching career. It may include people you look up to, inspiring quotes that keep you going especially on tough days, and words that define you and your values. It will remind you of the teacher you are now and the teacher you wanted to become in the first place.
4. Best and worst teacher analyses are another way to reflect. You can do this one alone or with a group of teachers. Think about your best teacher when you were a student. List the top five personal qualities, skills, or attitudes that made them so exceptional. Next, think of your worst teacher. List the top five personal qualities, skills, or attitudes that made them the worst teacher. Now make a list of qualities, skills, or attitudes you want to adopt or get rid of as a teacher yourself (Renard 2019).

For example, a new middle school principal, at one of her first school-wide assemblies, had to deal with rowdy and loud students who would not listen to a Shakespearean theater group. She went up to the microphone and calmly said she knew the students represented a fine middle school and they were very capable of listening to Shakespeare. After that, there was silence for the rest of the assembly. She accomplished what she needed to do without yelling at the students or shaming them. She was poised and calm.

Sometimes, when you are looking back and self-reflecting, it is helpful to break the lesson plan into its different components.

1. Preparation and Research: Were you well prepared? What were the sources of your information?
2. Written Plan: Were you organized? Was the lesson written in a methodical sequence, the next step building on the previous one?
3. Presentation: Were the students involved? Give evidence. Were you clear in your presentation? How was the pacing?
4. Assessment: Did the method of assessment measure what you wanted it to? How did the class do? Would you change the assess-

ment for the next time? ("Lesson Plan Self-Reflection and Evaluation" 2017).

For example, in the category of pacing, principals may sit through teacher evaluations with a stopwatch in their hand and clock how much time is spent on individual components. They might note a great lesson with excellent student rapport but notice the explanation of the concept lasted thirty minutes before the students broke into pairs to practice it. Make sure students have time to process smaller chunks of material and practice them, instead of having a lengthier explanation before they can apply and reinforce it.

Teach and practice with your students how to transition from one activity to the next one. State in your syllabus that transitions are always doing and never saying, unless students are specifically asked to talk. If you say to open the book to page 19, they open the book to page 19, period. They do not start talking about their weekend plans. Seamless transitions make more time for learning. You are teaching them to value learning.

If you save fifteen minutes a day through efficient transitions, the result is forty-five extra hours of instructional time per year. There are three types of transitions: entering class and taking a seat, switching from one academic activity to another, and exiting class. Transitions must be taught through explanations, models, practice, review, and reflection.

Standardize the transition process with five steps.

1. Get the students' attention. "Focus on me, please."
2. Explain the procedure. "In a moment, return to your desks and take out your history textbooks." "In a moment" implies wait and do not move yet.
3. Prepare the students for the signal to start. "When I say smooth, you will quietly proceed."
4. Initiate the transition. "Smooth." Never say "Go" because that word cues the students to race.
5. Observe. Watch to make sure all students are complying. (Finley 2017)

You could even teach students at the beginning of the year transitional words and accompanying hand signals you will use to go along with your commands. For example, when the students are involved in pair work, tell them the number of minutes they have for the activity and set the timer. The timer rings at the end of the activity. Say an appropriate command like, "Attention, class, silence please." Put your right index finger up to your lips.

Teach the students to freeze wherever they are in the class and give you immediate eye contact. This is a checkpoint: if all eyes are not looking at you, wait. Observe students nudging noncomplying classmates and pointing at you. Tell your students you will not raise your voice during a command to get their attention because the volume of the class should never get so loud the students cannot hear you.

The next command could be "In thirty seconds, in silence, return to your assigned seats." Your hand signal could be your hands rolling around each other. Set the timer, observe the students, and say nothing else during the actual transition. If the transition is not done correctly, repeat the command with your hand signal and have them practice it again.

If the transitions are taking too long or the students are not cooperating, you need to reflect on the situation. Are your directions too complicated or not specific enough? Were the students not warned of an upcoming transition and they were so caught up in an activity they had trouble tearing themselves away? Were there specific students who did not follow the directions?

If the transitions are taking too long, announce before the transition how many seconds they have for the transition, show them the timer, and follow through. They need to practice until they transition correctly. You could even make it a friendly competition and announce how long it took other classes to transition. Be patient. At the beginning of the year, this may take time to get right. Budget that into your lesson plan so you are not frustrated. It is well worth the extra time. Once it is ingrained and if you are consistent and insistent, this will be not be an issue. Practice it also after long vacation breaks.

If the procedures are not being followed, try reminders before a transition. Ask a student to describe the sequential steps the class needs to do before a specific command and then practice it as a class. Or play the game "Correct the Teacher." The teacher could have the students call out the command and the teacher models correct and incorrect responses. The students put their thumbs up or down to signal if the teacher's response was appropriate or not. Then call on a student and then the class to model the correct response.

Recapping, research shows successful transitions are quick and have clear beginnings and endings.

Have file cabinets by unit (and/or on your computer) where you keep a hard copy of each of your handouts, so you can find them quickly to copy for next year.

Be a lifelong learner and believe there is always something new to learn at every stage of your career. Go to workshops, read current research, pursue advanced degrees, attend professional development classes, and collaborate with your colleagues. As you learn more, you get more excited, and so do your students.

Post grades in a timely fashion. You should post at least one grade a week. An accountable teacher means more accountable students and fewer phone calls from parents.

When students do not know a grade on an assignment, they are more anxious than when they do know a grade. If they receive a good grade, they can move on. If they do not receive a good grade, they can figure out how do better next time or get help. If they do not know a grade, they worry about their ungraded past assignments instead of focusing on new material. With no feedback, they wonder if they failed or are learning what they are supposed to learn.

Some teachers are late grading students' assignments because they say they have large numbers of students or because the students do not read the feedback. They find assignments on the floor or in recycling bins (Corwin 2016).

The benefits of giving students quick feedback are worth the time and effort. If students do not receive feedback on their work, they cannot know what they did right or wrong. Therefore, they cannot learn from it. Assignments are a process toward a goal, so give feedback as part of the process. Frequent evaluations of student work help a teacher better assess the students' strengths and weaknesses. Students do best when teachers know them well. This way, the teacher can better guide them because they know what the student needs.

The online gradebook is the main line of communication between teachers, students, and parents. If teachers do not keep the gradebook up to date, students and parents do not know what kind of progress they are making or their current grade in the class. The number one complaint from parents is teachers not updating their gradebooks. Some students say when teachers fall behind in updating grades, students are not as motivated to keep up their work (Lam 2015).

Grade students' assignments immediately and put in their scores by the end of the day. Do this to keep your workload manageable. If you let things pile up, you will be more stressed out. For projects or lengthier tests, give yourself a week to grade them. Up-to-date grading shows you care about your students. You really want to know if they understand the material or not. Sometimes in a large classroom, you do not know this until you look at their individual work.

After you grade the homework, go over it the next day in class. Go around and help students you know are struggling, pair them with students who understand the material, or privately invite them to office hours for extra help. You will have a higher homework turn-in rate because your students know they will get immediate feedback. They also know you will not accept late assignments except for an excused absence or excused tardy.

There is a movement now to grade students' tests only to show mastery learning and not to grade assignments. This is a serious mistake. Only grading tests, teachers have less items to grade, but school becomes a product and not a process. The result is more important than the learning. Cheating goes way up because the tests are high stakes since they are the only grade that matters. This is the wrong message.

Teach students the value of homework. It takes discipline and patience to improve. It takes step-by-step feedback from teachers during lessons. You cannot skip to the final product, the test, without the process, the practice, and the homework.

Homework encourages the growth mindset: if you work at it, you can improve. Without homework, it is a fixed mindset, not giving yourself a chance to improve. You are either a natural at something and it comes easily to you, or you are not good at something and you will never improve.

You will encounter students who want to drop your class after the first week of school! They are not used to having to put in effort, so they just assume they are not good at your class subject. If they did that through their whole life, avoiding anything that takes effort, they would limit themselves to the familiar because growth involves moving out of their comfort zone.

In a 2011 online article, Robert Ryshke, executive director at the Center for Teaching at the Westminster Schools in Atlanta, Georgia, included the 2007 results of the MetLife Survey of the American Teacher: The Homework Experience. Answers came from 1,200 K–12 public-school teachers, 500 parents, and 2,000 students. Some of the findings were: most parents, students, and teachers believe homework is important and helps students learn at school. Fifty percent of teachers frequently use homework to help students practice skills, prepare for tests, develop good work habits, develop critical thinking skills, and get motivated to learn.

Highly experienced teachers (twenty-plus years of experience) are more likely than new teachers (five years or fewer of experience) to believe homework is important: it helps students learn more in school and it helps them reach their goals after high school. New teachers are less likely than highly experienced teachers to provide students with feedback on homework or to review completed assignments during class discussions.

Regular failure to complete homework assignments may be an early signal of student disengagement that can lead to school-related problems. Parents who do not believe homework is important appear to be less connected to their child's school. Seventy-five percent of students say they have enough time to do their assignments. The 25 percent who say they do not have enough time have higher rates of risk factors related to student achievement and other areas. Those who lack time for their homework are more likely to get low grades and are less likely to plan to go to college.

Ninety percent of parents say speaking with their child about their homework is an opportunity to spend time together. They do not see homework as a major source of stress getting in the way of family time. Eighty percent of parents say their child's teacher assigns the right amount of homework.

Ryshke believes homework should not be given unless the teacher gives feedback to their students. Homework should inform the teacher if their teaching has been effective and if the student has learned the material. Homework should be a part of the student's overall achievement grade because if it is methodically related to the current concepts being taught, it is a good indicator of student performance. Homework should have two purposes: assess student understanding and prepare students for future learning.

Ryshke also believes the school needs to set the homework guidelines and not let individual teachers set their own. That way, students' success is based on their performance and not on whether different teachers have different policies for how to manage homework (Ryshke 2011).

Some teachers believe they should be allowed their own homework, review, and test policies. If the school administration agrees, the specific policies must be stated in their syllabi. These teachers could tell their students every classroom is like visiting a different home, and you must follow the rules of that home. This is a life skill: you will have different bosses and different policies, and you need to learn how to deal with that now.

Some school departments are required to use the same categories and percentages for grading scale consistency purposes, but their own individual assignments are decided by the teacher. For example, a world languages department might use: assignments and quizzes: 25 percent of the overall grade, tests: 30 percent, self-assessing the tests: 5 percent, immersion in the target language: 15 percent, cultural projects once a semester: 5 percent, and final exam: 20 percent. This makes the point that homework is just as important as the test, hence 30 percent for tests and 25 percent for assignments. That way, if a student is a poor test taker, they can still pass the class if they are putting in the effort to do the assignments.

Assign brief homework assignments several times a week. Make them due the next day, collect them at the beginning of class, grade them while the students have individual seat work, return them during that same class period, and go over them. Have unannounced quizzes about a week into new material, so the students know to study what you went over in class nightly, even if you did not assign homework every night.

After you return tests, go over them as a class. The students need to correct all their errors in red pen, write a self-reflection, and return the test to you to receive full credit in the category of self-assessment.

The self-reflection piece could mean students look over the test and then finish sentences you provide. For example, "The hardest part of the test was . . . ," "The easiest part of the test was . . . ," "I prepared for this test by . . . ," "Something new I learned from this test was . . ." Students actually have to finish your sentences with concepts like "vocabulary," "how to write a complete sentence," "reviewing my notes," "the present perfect tense and how to conjugate it and use it in a letter." Do not accept "section A" or "section B." You want the students to use critical thinking to figure out their answers.

Have the students self-assess the test so they will not just look at the grade and throw the test out. You want them to learn from it. If they throw the test out and do not return it to you, they receive a zero for the self-assessment. While you go over the test, if the student catches an error in the grading on your part, tell them to write you a note at the top of their test, and when the tests are returned to you, tell them if you agree, they will see a grade change. Do not allow students to focus on their grade and complain aloud about it during class. Class time is to focus on student learning.

As far as grading assignments, write in your syllabus that you grade for completion sometimes and accuracy other times. By not telling the students beforehand, it keeps them on their toes and makes grading easier for you. For projects, give them a rubric ahead of time of your specific expectations.

For tests, tell them which pages from the text or which notes to study. Give them a pretest a week before the test with the same content but different questions on the test. After the pretest, announce that during the test, you will allow one prewritten index card if the material is difficult; other times tell them they cannot use notes on a test. If you allow an index card, check during the test they are using one card only and not sharing it with another student. Have them turn in their index card with their finished test.

Never let students write on their tests if you will be using them with multiple classes. When they finish, have students come to you individually with their tests and answer sheets, so you can account for all tests. Thumb through the tests. If they write on the tests, deduct a few points. Make sure this is stated in your syllabus. When students get used to this procedure, it will continue for all tests, including final exams. This will save you time from having to reprint tests and waste school paper due to answers on the tests.

In a 2019 online article by Seattle teacher Jenna Vandenberg, entitled "Why Homework Matters: It's Not Just About Grades," she writes of the growing trend of elementary schools to not assign homework because some research has shown it to be ineffective or because of an equity gap. Specifically, low-income students spend less time on take-home assignments.

She argues homework is a habit that needs to be developed early on because when a student reaches high school and suddenly has homework for more advanced content-driven classes, they will not have the motivation or skills to do it, since it was never expected of them before. They do not know how to set aside time and complete a task outside of school, and struggle through problems when a teacher or classmate is not around. In other words, they have not learned to be independent (Vandenberg 2019).

Schools now emphasize group work and collaboration. This is a needed skill for the workplace, but workers also must be able to work alone, think for themselves, and finish a project. The National Education Association Parents' Guide still recommends ten to twenty minutes of homework a day for K–2 students and increasing that amount ten minutes a year. Harris Cooper, an education researcher says, "The average correlation between time spent on homework and achievement was substantial for secondary students. . . . For high school students, the positive line continues to climb until between 90 minutes and 2.5 hours of homework a night."

As far as equity, students in lower-income families may not have as much parental presence since the parents may be working multiple jobs to support the family. Homework may provide the structure needed to practice academic knowledge and vocabulary and keep them focused on their education.

When all students get to high school, regardless of socioeconomic status, parents tend to step away, as they want their children to take on more responsibilities. If the students have not learned how to do homework because they never had to until high school, how will they suddenly make it a habit with less parental involvement? Homework is not just about grades: it is about ingraining an independent skill that will help students succeed in life.

There is also another trend right now of a no-zero grading policy so the lowest possible grade for any assignment or test is 50 percent—even when the student turns in no work at all. School districts in favor of it say it gives all students a chance to succeed. They believe low grades encourage struggling students to give up. When they receive an F, they tend to withdraw, try less, and come to school less because they feel like they are failures and do not fit into the school environment. When grades are a punishment for not following the rules instead of a demonstration of mastery of assessment, they lose their value.

However, some school districts, like Leominster Public Schools in Massachusetts, have done away with the no-zero grading policy after years of doing it because the students were not learning to be responsible. While teachers at that school reported zeros could dampen enthusiasm for learning, they said the no-zero policy had the same effect with possible long-term consequences.

A no-zero grading policy allowed students who had not mastered the content to be moved ahead. When they came up against a harder subject, the next grade level, or college, they were unprepared and dug themselves deeper into a hole. Not letting a child go ahead is not punishment. It is helping a child. It is making sure the child is prepared before moving on to the next step.

In the 1960s, at the end of the school year, it was a big deal when students received their report card. It said at the bottom if they were officially promoted or not and was signed by their teacher. Children left the building in tears. They survived. They came back the next fall and repeated the grade. That does not happen now. Society worries about the child's self-esteem. But is it worse to keep pushing a child through the system when they are not up to grade level?

Veteran high school teacher Thomas Bannan said, "We are creating a generation of entitled people who are hitting colleges and the job market with major holes in their abilities to survive." Teacher Lara Morales said, "Zeros do not create holes. Kids choosing not to do their work creates holes." NBCT (nationally board-certified teacher) Ray Salazar said, "We've gotten to a point where we save students academically instead of teaching them how to save themselves" (Salazar 2019; Minero 2018).

When posting grades on the Internet for an assignment, test, or quiz, if a student has not taken them for any reason, put a zero next to their name. This reminds you they have not completed the assignment. If it was an excused absence or tardy, once they complete the assignment, change the zero to their earned grade. If you just leave the space blank, the grade is not counted against them. The zero creates a sense of urgency for the student to get rid of it. Make sure this policy is stated in your syllabus at the beginning of the year.

According to a 2018 online article by middle school teacher Sheldon Soper entitled "The Implications of Grading without Zeros," one of the largest problems of the no-zero grading policy was a lessening of student accountability. Accountability is a life skill to be successful. Life has deadlines that, if not met, can carry serious consequences. The no-zero grade policy sends the message that doing nothing is still rewarded (Soper 2018).

In a 2013 online article entitled "Solving the Problems of Zeros in Grading," Dr. Thomas Guskey, a senior research scholar in the College of Education at the University of Louisville, said the problem was not the minimum grades or the zero, but the percentage grading system: "In a percentage grading system, to move from a B to an A generally requires improvement of 10%, say 80% to 90%. But to move from zero to a minimum passing grade requires six to seven times that improvement, usually zero to 60%. Two-thirds of the marks in a percentage grading system denote levels of failure. Only one-third of the marks are considered passing.

The solution is to do away with percentages in grading and use integers instead: 0–4. Some U.S. colleges and universities use the 0–4 system. In the integer system, a student receives a zero when they do not turn in work. To improve from a zero to a passing grade means to move from zero to one, not from zero to 60 percent. This makes it possible for a student to recover (Guskey 2013).

New is not always the best. The goal is purposeful teaching. Do not mistake fads for innovative teaching. For example, a school was in a one-hundred-member faculty meeting. They were randomly assigned into smaller groups of five people. They were asked what the ideal classroom would look like. The immediate answer was lots of technology. But as they dove deeper, they recognized technology was a tool, like textbooks. It did not get to the heart of the question: the culture of the classroom.

This is difficult because teachers are being told by the latest research not to lead but to facilitate. Parents want their kids to come home loving school and not stressing the parents out. Students want learning with no effort and no homework. This simply is not possible. Teachers need to lead, parents need to parent, and students need to learn.

What is the purpose of education? Why even send children to school? Education is to prepare students to enter society as productive, responsible, and empathetic adults. To accomplish this, stakeholders need to stay focused on student learning and student civility.

Student civility means a student thinks beyond themselves and pushes outward toward others in their community, their country, and the world.

For example, expect students to show respect to others in the classroom and beyond and to listen to others as they share their views.

Most schools have two separate categories of grades per subject: the academic grade and the citizenship or behavioral grade. Districts have warned teachers the behavior of the student cannot affect the academic grade. Teachers have tried to get around that with a participation grade as part of the academic grade, but many schools have forbidden that as well. High school transcripts report academic grades only to colleges and not the citizenship grade.

Salvatore Babones, an American sociologist, writes that American education emphasizes academic achievement only. However, he feels "education is primarily about good citizenship and not academic learning."

> All those hours spent in classrooms should be used to help our children grow into happy, productive, moral, responsible, reasonably well-behaved adults who care deeply about our communities, our country, and the world. Subjects like art, music, and the theater are just as important for civility as are subjects like English, Science, and Math.
>
> America isn't a place: it's a people. All Americans have a stake in shaping what the next generation will be like, even people who do not have children. That is why even people who do not have children support local public schools, staffed by professionals who know their students and care about their communities. . . . The federal government should entrust states and communities to bring up good citizens and give them the resources to do so. States should trust their counties. And counties their towns.
>
> It may go against political nature to provide funding without demanding measurable outcomes, but good citizenship is not measurable. A progressive President who is not beholden to the for-profit education industry can . . . return America's public schools to public management in the public service.
>
> Education reform has focused on turning schools into knowledge factories: teach more, study more, test more, and everything else, less. The data show the knowledge factory model of education has not improved American test scores, which have been essentially unchanged since 1971. Countries like Finland that embed schools in the community do much better on standardized tests than we do. (Babones 2015)

One of the best ways to teach students to be empathetic is through global education. In a 2016 online article by David Young, CEO of VIF, Visiting International Faculty, now called Participate, an organization dedicated to providing collaborative and continuous learning opportunities to empower teachers and inspire students, the term "global education" was defined.

Global education is "an interdisciplinary approach to learning concepts and skills necessary to function in a world that is increasingly interconnected and multicultural. The curricula based on this approach are grounded in traditional academic disciplines but are taught in the context of project and problem-based inquiries."

Through global education, students and teachers gain global competence. Global competence is "a dynamic term that includes in-depth knowledge and understanding of international issues, an appreciation of and ability to learn and work with people from diverse linguistic and cultural backgrounds, proficiency in a foreign language, and skills to function productively in an interdependent world community" (Young 2016).

Becoming proficient in a foreign language (also referred to as world language) according to the American Council on the Teaching of Foreign Languages (ACTFL) means "the ability to use language in real world situations on a spontaneous interaction and non-rehearsed context and in a manner acceptable and appropriate to native speakers of the language" (Berdan 2020). Proficiency is not fluency: proficiency is the capacity to understand and speak enough to have a meaningful conversation; fluency is to be able to communicate flawlessly at the level of a native speaker.

In the United States, getting to the level of foreign language proficiency has been a hard sell. US students are encouraged to learn a foreign language because it could benefit success in school, future careers, and overall brain development and intelligence. And even then, only a third of Americans believe knowing a language is important for success in today's economy. Only 50 percent of US citizens own a passport.

Preparing students for their future careers is an important goal of education, but another goal is to prepare students to be good citizens, build relationships with others, and positively contribute to society.

In a 2019 article entitled "Reevaluating the Importance of Foreign Languages," Katherine Stark interviewed students at Michigan State University on why they took classes in foreign language. These students viewed learning as an essential public good: beyond benefiting themselves, it benefited the world. Most students said it resulted in a personal transformation because it made them more interested in connecting with other people, and not just using English and expecting the other person to know English so they could connect with them. They also learned to appreciate other cultures by learning another language.

It increased their empathy and appreciation for others in the United States whose first language was not English. After these MSU students learned how hard it was to learn a new language, they did not put down newcomers to the United States who were struggling in the process. They could understand the frustration of being unable to communicate what was on their mind because they went through that in their language classes or when they visited a country where English was not the official language of the country.

This increase in empathy went beyond one-on-one interactions. They now saw themselves as global citizens. They saw themselves united with people different than themselves because of their shared humanity. When these students listened or read the news, they no longer only paid attention to what affected them, but they broadened their focus: they now cared about natural disasters or civil wars around the globe (Stark 2019).

The benefits of global education are appreciation of culture, evaluation of information, cross-cultural communication skills, perspective-taking skills, intelligent humility, divergent thinking, and technological literacy.

Appreciation of culture: When you travel to another country, you may come back appreciating your own culture more and not take things for granted. For example, toilet paper in every bathroom in the United States does not exist in every country. You may also learn from another culture ideas you want to incorporate into your culture; for example, the love and dedication to extended family in the Mexican culture and how the elderly relatives are held in high esteem and looked to for guidance. They continue to live with their family in their later years and are not sent off to nursing homes.

Evaluation of information: It is so easy to draw an opinion of Mexico, especially if you have never been there, by just reading an article put out by the media. Do you ever stop to think your opinion is influenced by your own culture? You need to question articles you read, look at the sources, read a variety of articles on the same topic, and not just accept one opinion at face value.

Cross-cultural communication skills: When you exchange ideas with peers and adults from different backgrounds—either virtually or in-person—you feel more comfortable and have the skills to enter unfamiliar communities and spaces. You feel braver and more open to exploration. You may want to travel internationally. There is a whole exciting world beyond you.

You realize your world at home is so small. Maybe the travel bug will catch on with your children, spouse, and students after they hear and see photos or PowerPoints of your adventures. Maybe they will feel if you can do it, so can they. You return a more open and empathetic person—perhaps traits they want too.

Perspective-taking skills: If you visit another country, try to arrange to live with a family. Taking formal courses is great, but you will get even more up close and personal. You will observe the family's commonalities and differences to your culture daily. You will learn about yourself and your reactions to these cultural similarities and differences. Can you look beyond yourself, not make snap judgments, and see it from their point of view? Can you ask questions out of curiosity to learn more about their culture?

They will be curious about you too. Can they see things from your point of view? Can they ask you questions about your culture and you answer without getting offended?

You will learn some things are universal and transcend cultures like love and acceptance; the family may "adopt" you as part of the family and call you their son or daughter and include you in family celebrations.

Intelligent humility: You may be humbled trying to communicate with the family in their native language and quickly realize you do not know everything. At first, you might act like you understand them to avoid admitting you do not. As you grow to trust them and accept your limitations, your language skills can improve.

You may also be frustrated and exhausted from your effort to speak their language and want them to come to you and speak your language. But then you are missing out on an opportunity to grow and experience another language, another culture, and another perspective. Try to embrace the uncomfortable, and if it gets overwhelming, give yourself a break, call friends and speak in English, but then go back and try again.

Divergent thinking: When you return to the United States, based on your experiences abroad, you might reflect on: What does your culture value? Does the other culture value it in the same or in a different way? For example, the US culture is always in a hurry. Time is a precious commodity. Birthday invitations read the exact time of a party from start to finish. Often activities are planned down to the minute.

In Mexico, birthday parties go on for hours. Extended families of twenty relatives or more come over armed with food and spend the next eight hours eating, singing, and talking. There is no sense of scheduled activities. The US culture would not go for this, but what if the US culture reconnected with their extended families more regularly? If the US culture were more connected to others besides their nuclear family, if they could extend more kindness to others, could that result in more kindness in the US culture?

Technological literacy: Now that you are reaching beyond your culture, you may be motivated to try new technology to communicate and collaborate with other cultures. It may be personal, like using Zoom or WhatsApp to have a video conversation, or more overreaching, like following news sources from other countries.

Eighty percent of teachers agree it is more important than ever to learn about other countries and cultures. But only 30 percent say they often use material about other countries and cultures in their lesson plans. Nearly six in ten teachers say this is due to lack of resources or administrative support but not due to lack of student support.

Nine in ten US students recognize jobs are becoming increasingly international, and they could be competing with other people around the world for the same job. They know they would be stronger candidates with a better understanding of different cultures. However, they also feel their enthusiasm for global education has not been met with an adequate level of instruction in global studies.

Sixty percent of secondary students ranked understanding different cultures the most important subject area, ahead of writing and math skills. Fifty percent of US students study a world language. Ninety percent of European students study at least one world language (Participate Learning 2016).

Another issue is not every student has equal access to global education. David Young, CEO of VIF, wrote in a 2014 online article entitled "Global Education for Every Student" that global education currently is for the privileged few. Unless you are on a university or college campus, a well-funded school district with an International Baccalaureate program (IB), or attending a private school committed to global themes, you probably will not find it.

This represents an opportunity gap. This means factors like race, ethnicity, socioeconomic status, English proficiency, community wealth, or other factors continue lower educational aspirations, achievement, and attainment for certain groups of students. All students are equally deserving of educational experiences that prepare them to be globally competent. We all live in the same interconnected world (Young 2014).

McQueen High School in Reno, Nevada, is not an IB school, yet it has global education courses and certification because an administrator at the school decided it was important. They traveled to China to learn more about it. McQueen High School became the Global Studies Signature Academy for the school district.

The Academy offers two programs: international studies and fine arts. For international studies, students are immersed in course work dealing with world politics, economics, ecological balance, global interaction and diplomacy, and international understanding. During this four-year course of study, students study two world languages, AP Human Geography, AP US History, AP American Government, AP Comparative Government, Economics, and AP Environmental Science. For fine arts, students are immersed in course work dealing with music and visual art.

-McQueen High School offers world language study in French, German, Mandarin Chinese, and Spanish. Students attend lectures on global issues by worldwide experts at the local university. Students graduate with a diploma in global studies. Their final project is presented in one of the world languages they learned on a world social or environmental issue.

McQueen High School Global Studies students were asked in a survey how the program helped them grow as a student and as a person. Here are some of their answers:

- "I have become more future-conscious."
- "It has made me challenge myself and strive to be better."
- "By implementing cultural elements into the curriculum and giving me opportunities to meet with people from all over the world, I am

convinced that I am having a much richer high school experience than most kids."
- "The required global studies classes have taught me more than the content: they have taught me how to be responsible, punctual, and hardworking. I have learned to view myself as a global instead of an American citizen."
- "It has helped me realize there is more going on than we often see in our daily lives. It has helped me think about the bigger picture."
- "I have made new friends and connections that I would not have made if I had not been in this program. It has allowed me to branch out."

Global education can use the existing infrastructure of schools and classrooms for global education and competence. New courses, new standards, and new models of learning are not needed. It must be intentional and built into the daily curriculum. Global education is not an occasional add-on.

Nichola Turner, a global studies elementary school teacher, models cultural appreciation for her students. She honors her students by using their backgrounds and interests within her curriculum. The three fundamental elements to Turner's teaching style are: (1) She is curious about her students' backgrounds. (2) She weaves her students' cultural and language heritages into her instruction. She obtains this information by having every student write a cultural résumé. (3) She dedicates instructional time to honoring her students' interests (Knight 2016).

In 1992, Spanish was referred to as a foreign language in course descriptions. The emphasis was on written grammar and culture was fluff. Maybe Mexico was thrown in through a grammar exercise but not as a cultural goal. Spain, South America, the Caribbean, and the Philippines were not mentioned. They had no relevance because people from the United States were not traveling there frequently. Also, technology was not where it is today, connecting the world.

The few Spanish teachers who did incorporate culture into their teachings felt they had to because they believed culture could not be divorced from grammar. They were concerned the big tests were grammar based only. They required their students to speak in Spanish only in the classroom because they did not want their students to study a language but to live and experience the language.

They came up with creative activities to apply the language like an annual evening puppet show for students and their parents. The students wrote their original scripts in Spanish and created sock puppets during class time. During the show, only the introduction was spoken in English. The actual skits were all in Spanish. Therefore, the students also learned how to use expression in their voices and actions with their puppets to communicate their stories to parents who did not know the language.

In later years, when Spanish was referred to as a world language instead of a foreign language, classroom immersion was more the norm than the exception. Some high school Spanish teachers required their students to present two memorized cultural projects every year in Spanish with a visual component. The visual, usually a PowerPoint, could have photos but no words. Some students did a live concert with Spanish guitars or danced a flamingo dance. The first semester they chose a Spanish theme and Hispanic country of their choice.

They could also choose a non-Hispanic country. Some students chose their heritage. For example, one student reported on Iran and another about Pakistan. It was an eye opener to learn about the rich culture of artists and musicians in these countries, something not generally known to US-born students.

The second semester the students chose a Hispanic food and had to present the memorized recipe and directions with a visual component. Usually that was the food itself. Students sampled grasshoppers from Mexico, pepper cookies from Iceland, lumpia from the Philippines, arepas from Colombia, and alfajores from Argentina. As the students presented in front of the class, the other students had to write down questions for them about their projects.

When the presentation ended, teachers randomly called upon students to ask their questions, and the presenters had to answer on the spot. All of this was done in Spanish. The current AP exams have a cultural as well as a grammar component.

Seattle's John Stanford International School (JSIS) is a global education elementary school. They have language immersion for half of the day in Japanese or Spanish. The other half of the day instruction is in English. They discuss social issues, and they act on them. Teachers must be experienced in global education, have language skills, participate in PLCs, and be lifelong learners.

Nicole Silver, a teacher at JSIS, says to build on what you care about to turn it into global education. For example, she took a traditional unit on winter festivals where in the past, students would be taught about three holidays. Now she has the students choose one winter festival from around the world, raise questions through the inquiry process, conduct research, and think critically about issues of religious tolerance. She has students think about whether they have ever felt like an outsider. "What was it like not to fit in?" As an action step, "How do we welcome everyone?"

Use parents as global resources. At the beginning of the year, JSIS kindergarten and first-grade teacher Julie Colando surveys parents about their careers. If any of them work outside of the United States, she invites them as guest speakers to her classroom. She says the presentations are like mini–TED talks but geared for five- and six-year-olds.

Parents have presented on topics like oceanography, vaccines, and sanitation in the developing world. One parent, whose topic was clean water issues, began with showing photos of homes, food, toys, and toilets around the world. He asked the students what they noticed in the photos. Without judging other cultures, he asked the students, "What if you could not wash your hands? What if there were no bathrooms? What might happen to your drinking water?"

Nicole Silver changes her global curriculum every year to keep it fresh not only for herself but for her students. She starts the year by connecting with her current students' experiences. She asks them where they are from and what are their prior experiences. If she has immigrant or English-language learners, she wants to know what they can teach their American-born classmates about other cultures (Teaching Global Competence 2013).

A fantastic opportunity for U.S. elementary, middle school, and high school educators is Fulbright's Teachers for Global Classrooms Program (Fulbright TGC). Educators are chosen to participate in a yearlong professional learning opportunity and a two- or three-week visit to locations around the world to learn about the educational systems and cultures in different countries so they can return and prepare their students for a competitive global economy and global collaboration with other countries.

In one of the TGC webinars, Dr. William Gaudelli, the author of *Global Citizenship Education*, asked U.S. educators, "Who are you?"

Participants were instructed to write in the chat box the first two words that popped into their head. Some educators wrote, "Jewish and female." Others wrote, "Teacher and humanitarian." He said that is your self-identity and the lens through which you see the world. He next asked, "Where are you?" Participants were instructed to write in the chat box the first word that popped into their head. Some educators wrote, "Earth." Others said, "Home" or "Nevada." What a great exercise!

Try this with your own students at the beginning of the year to demonstrate how their identity effects their perspective of the world. What if a person responded, "Black and male"? How could that affect how they see the world? To put yourself in someone else's shoes for a moment makes you realize everyone does not see the world as you do.

Another great global educational program to get involved in is the Fulbright Teaching Excellence and Achievement Program (TEA). It is hosted at a some US universities around the country.

International teachers observe and coteach in English with a host teacher in US classrooms for six weeks. If they go into a world language class, they can speak in the target language of that classroom. They also guest speak in other classes at that school and other schools in the district. These TEA teachers come in all shapes and colors from countries all around the world.

One day a male teacher from Africa was a guest speaker. He asked students how they would describe him. The students turned to look nervously at their teacher, and there was dead silence. He gently laughed and said they would describe him as Black, and not to be afraid to say that out loud.

He had a beautiful PowerPoint that included facts and photos about Africa. Afterward, the students asked him questions about the teenagers in Africa: How did they dress? What music did they listen to? What were the schools like in Africa? The students could have read these facts in a book, but it is not the same as having a live speaker converse directly with them. Students later said they were fascinated with Africa and might want to visit there someday.

Nicole Silver said another reason to keep curriculum fresh is you can respond to current global events. During an election year, her students participated in a mock election. They also investigated voting rights around the world and evaluated information sources for reliability. Silver asks thought-provoking prompts no matter the topic. For example,

"What's the world like outside my experience? How could I find out? How can we listen to and learn from others?"

For additional resources about teaching global education, download a free copy of *Educating for Global Competence: Preparing Our Youth to Engage the World* (http://asiasociety.org/files/book-globalcompetence.pdf) by Veronica Boix Mansilla and Anthony Jackson.

After the JSIS read and discussed this book as a staff, they felt more prepared to plan units that "emphasized principles such as teaching students to recognize and express their own perspectives, examine the perspectives of others, and act in ethical and creative ways to improve the world" ("Teaching Global Competence" 2013).

Why was there no toilet paper in the bathrooms in Mexico and Colombia? Why if you brought your own should it be deposited in the adjacent garbage can instead of flushed down the toilet? Instead of judging them, research the answer. It turns out the pipes are old and narrow and there is low water pressure. They just cannot handle paper products. Also, some people steal the toilet paper, so it is not provided.

Another reason for global education is to educate against racism. Racism can be found in schools in student-to-student interaction, student-to-teacher interaction, teacher-to-teacher interaction, educational access and funding, teacher preparedness, and school discipline. Racism is a learned behavior. With effort, education, and action, racism can be prevented and addressed in schools.

To help prevent racism, educators must be self-aware. They must understand how their identification within a group gives them privilege in certain situations, and they must actively listen to marginalized groups who have a different life experience because of their social grouping. They must acknowledge their own biases and try to understand people with different life experiences.

School faculties in the United States do not represent cultural diversity. Cultural diversity means beyond color and ethnicity and includes customs, religious experiences, political views, sexual orientation, and more. Referencing color for example, today 80 percent of public-school teachers are White and over 45 percent of public-school students are in the minority populations.

A diverse faculty is important for students and faculty. First, students need role models with a common background to give them a sense of belonging and comfort, so they can relate to their teacher better. Second, a diverse faculty will expose students to a wide array of ideas, cultures, and individuals. The more diverse the faculty, the more diverse the course content, curriculum, teaching methods, and unique experiences brought to the classroom. All of this can improve the effectiveness of teaching.

Third, a diverse faculty prepares students for the world because it shows students how to communicate and work with all types of people after they leave school. Fourth, there are less discrimination claims because if educators know an educational institution openly hires a diverse faculty, they will more likely want to work for that institution and less likely to be discriminated against.

Once diverse staff are hired, it must be an ongoing effort to retain them. A 2005 University of Pennsylvania study by Richard Ingersoll found that teachers of color left the profession 24 percent more often than White teachers. Teachers of color must feel welcome at their schools. A site-based professional development where the staff share their backgrounds and family histories might make the entire staff feel more comfortable, included, and connected to their coworkers. It might reduce assumptions the staff make of each other based on limited daily interactions.

University teacher preparation programs can prepare future teachers for a diverse student population by having their candidates engage with diverse students and contexts through well-designed field experiences (Segaren 2019).

Teachers can be biased toward students of different races. In a 2016 online article by Melinda Anderson entitled "How Discrimination Shapes Parent-Teacher Communication," she wrote about the Education Longitudinal Study of 2002, a nationwide sampling conducted by the US Department of Education. This study involved ten thousand mainly public high school sophomores, their parents, and teachers. It showed the role students' race and country of birth play in a teacher's likelihood of contacting the parents or guardians.

In the category of behavioral problems, according to this 2002 Educational Longitudinal Study, teachers were more likely to call Black and Latino parents than Caucasian parents. Black and Latino students were stereotyped with more discipline issues. Teachers were less likely to call Black or Latino parents over academic concerns because the teachers felt these students were not capable of understanding the material or their parents probably were apathetic about their child's education.

Teachers were less likely to call Asian parents over academic and behavioral struggles because they were viewed as hardworking and well-behaved. This is known as the "model minority" myth that Asian students are always compliant (Anderson 2016).

One reason some teachers are reluctant to enact early intervention discipline of Black or Latino students until it gets out of control and they must call the parents is because the teacher fears being called a racist by the student. If a student labels you as racist in front of the class, take that student outside of the classroom immediately and let them know their word choice is not appropriate. Give them the opportunity to rejoin the class and not blurt out again. If they indicate that will not work for them, send them to the office and document what happened during class.

If their parent calls you a racist, say to the parent you are sorry they feel that way, but the issue here is student accountability and responsibility for their own actions. For example, if a student chooses to regularly blurt out during class, then the behavioral consequences stated in your syllabus will apply to any student. Do not back down. You oversee your class.

On the other hand, if a teacher is using racially inappropriate language, they must be held accountable and this must be reported to the school administration because it interferes with student learning and is unprofessional. Teachers are role models for their students.

Educators need to attend professional development classes to increase their cultural competence. You see the world through your limited view. Courses are also needed on culturally relevant teaching, diversity, and multiculturalism. Also, if possible, educators need to travel to other countries. Challenge yourself and visit countries where the main race is not Caucasian and the main language is not English.

For example, most people in Colombia are not Caucasian. One day in Colombia, little children shouted out, "Gringos!" when they saw a group of White teachers. Some of the White teachers, not used to being called a derogatory word for White people when they were in the United States, were offended. These children were not used to seeing White people. Perhaps they blurted out an unfiltered reaction with a term they had learned at some point.

The first day of high school, students were asked to list four coping actions they could take if they were in a city where no English was spoken. The students were very resourceful. They said use gestures, draw, make sounds, or purchase an English to the new language dictionary/online translator. Nowadays you can even scan a menu with your cell phone in the original language and it will convert to the desired language.

Culturally relevant teaching is needed where race and ethnicity are acknowledged, where mainstream historical events are viewed through the lens of different racial groups.

Explicit lessons on racism and conflict resolutions are needed. These discussions can be uncomfortable, but with proper teacher preparation from professional development classes, they can be growth experiences for everyone.

Teachers need awareness of how racial bias impacts discipline. According to the US Education Department's Civil Rights Data Collection, Black students are suspended or expelled three times the rate of their White peers for the same offenses (Vagins 2014).

Schools need to partner with community organizations who are dealing with issues of racism and equity in the community and preventing them with social justice. Also, invite families into the classroom to talk about their experiences with racism to show this is real and not just hypothetical stories from a textbook (Bennett 2018).

In 2019, the European Commission Against Racism and Intolerance (ECRI) wrote an online article entitled "Combating Racism and Discrimination in and through Education." Evelyne Heyer, professor of the National Museum of Natural History of France, said the DNA of all humans is 99.9 percent identical and everyone is of African origin. With only 0.1 percent of differences in the genomes of people worldwide, the issue of race is not justifiable. "Racism is not just about skin color, but about discrimination against individuals who are physically, culturally, or morally different." She explained our genetic diversity is because of adaptations to environments and our geographical origins.

Three components that define racism are: categorization, hierarchization, and essentialization. Categorization is when people simplify the world by putting people in categories by their appearance, their religion, their geographic origin, and so forth. Hierarchization is a value judgment regarding one group or category of individuals as being superior or inferior to another. Essentialization is when individuals are reduced to moral characteristics, intellectual faculties. or psychological traits that are said to be permanent and an inherited feature of that group ("Combating Racism and Discrimination in and through Education" 2019).

Sometimes students come to this country and their parents try to blend them into the customs of Caucasians; for example, only speaking English at home with their children or changing their children's names to American names. Unfortunately, that sometimes means losing their identities. This is a personal decision, but in more recent years, children proudly speak their native tongue at home and do keep their original names with the original sound pronounced and spelled phonetically in English.

To prepare for Fulbright Teachers for Global Classrooms, the selected teachers had to complete a rigorous global training that included articles, online chat boards, and webinars. James Banks, the founding director of the Banks Center for Educational Justice, wrote an article about implementing global education into the curriculum. He advocated representation of all cultural groups within a nation, so no one needed to protest for their individual interests.

He wanted the focus on global identification instead of individual interests. He used history as evidence. He said in the past citizenship education embraced assimilation where everyone tried to fit into the Anglo Protestant conception of the "good citizen." As a result, parents did not teach their children their first culture, language, or ethnic identity, so the children could fit in (Banks 2008, 129–139).

This occurs sometimes in world language classes. The Hispanic child comes to class with no previous knowledge of Spanish. What is interesting is that when they go home and report what they learned in Spanish class, the student returns to class the next day and tells their teacher that their parents disagreed with the vocabulary word the teacher taught the student for an object.

Rita Izsak-Ndiaye, a member of the Committee on the Elimination of Racial Discrimination, says the fight against racial discrimination begins at home. She believes parents need to teach their children love, tolerance of others, and not to remain silent when there are acts of racism. "Everyone owns society. Education, arts, music, literature and science need to include everyone" ("Combating Racism and Discrimination in and through Education" 2019).

Leave detailed substitute plans. You need a break, so take it. Your goal is to come back and carry on without missing a beat. You do not want extra stress from parents, teachers, administrators, or your sub regarding problems in the classroom while you were gone. Therefore, put time into your substitute preparation. Do leave seating charts with the students' pictures on them, if possible. That way, they cannot change seats to sit with their friends. Do leave lesson plans on the board; e-mailed to your head secretary, if required; and for the sub, in case the plans get erased from the board.

Do hold the students responsible. Write in your syllabus and on the board the day you are absent that they must pass forward all assigned work at the end of the class period. They may not take it home—even if they do not finish it. This is your proof they were on task during class. Do grade the papers, for completion or certain sections for accuracy. Mix it up, just like regular homework grading, so the students are always held accountable for all their work. Do return the papers right away and use it as a review of what they did on the sub day.

If possible, do not leave plans that involve technology. The technology may not work, and this leaves the sub in a very vulnerable position of missed class learning. By the time someone is found to fix the situation, the class is over or on to off-task learning. Instead, assign work out of the textbook or worksheets. This is another reason to use the textbook at appropriate times in your classroom, so the students are used to and value it and do not see it as busy work with a substitute teacher.

If possible, have the students work alone. If they must work in pairs or small groups, hold them accountable. Tell them they will receive the same group grade per group and all names of the group members must be on the papers. Do write on the board that no technology will be seen or heard in class that day. If you have trained your students, you will have few students who will not follow this daily rule. Do follow through with consequences. Tell the sub to write down specific names of students who violated the rules. Do talk with these students individually before or after class immediately when you return, but never punish an entire class.

For safety, leave your policy about passes outside of the classroom for your sub. For example, each student has three passes per semester. Teach your students the procedure for using their passes. For example, remain seated, raise your hand, and get permission from the teacher. Then you the teacher or the substitute teacher writes it in the attendance binder. Students must turn in their cell phones before they go to the bathroom and pick it up upon return to the classroom. Once they have used three passes, write it next to their name on your seating chart to remind you they are done for the semester.

Tell students at the beginning of the year if they have a health issue at any point during the year where they need to use the bathroom more frequently, you need a note from their doctor or parents.

Never let more than one student out of your classroom at the same time. Students could plan meet-ups and miss out on learning. If a student is gone a long time, ask them why. That could end their passes for the semester. Remember you are legally responsible for them during your class period. Emergencies do happen, so use your best judgment, but they are rare and not on a regular basis for an individual student, or you need a note.

If one of the classes you oversee is study hall and a student tells you another teacher needs them to make up a quiz, tell them this must be prearranged by the teacher sending you an e-mail ahead of time that you approve.

Subs are in short supply now, so your goal is to have subs who want to sub for you when you need a day off. Remember, supply specific plans, students turn in work at the end of class, and they work individually, if possible.

3

PART OF THE TEAM: BENEFITS

Yes, you need to be a rule follower! When you follow the school rules, there is consistency among the staff and less chance for students to find the loopholes. Your life is much easier because you avoid problems with the administration and other staff members. Dress professionally. Just like you would be uncomfortable and less trusting if your doctor showed up in shorts and a T-shirt to your appointment, you need to refrain from that, unless you are the physical education teacher. You are a role model. The rules for student dress apply to you also.

Female teachers need to avoid wearing low-cut tops and skirts with high slits, and male teachers need to avoid shorts, T-shirts, and baseball hats. Students can be distracted from learning because students or faculty are dressed inappropriately.

Remember every child has the right to learn. If a student comes to your room dressed inappropriately, stop them before they enter the classroom and have them go back to their locker and get a sweater. If they do not have one, send them to the student relations office.

Hats in the classroom or the hallways are a danger: they can block people's faces. A nonstudent would be immediately recognized without a hat but may not be recognized as quickly with a hat.

Do all required supervisorial duties during the school day such as attending assemblies and sitting with your class and being in the hallway between classes. This not only shows respect to your administration but also keeps the school running smoothly.

Be at school during your required hours. If you must leave early, sign out. Be at all required IEP and 504 meetings after school. Your presence is required and your input essential. Decisions made at the meeting must be followed, regardless of if you were at the meeting or not.

If you want to make a difference and set yourself apart from other teachers, do it within the rules. Bending the rules to be the cool and popular teacher will cause issues for you and is unprofessional. Every day cannot be fun and games. Your job is to teach and not to entertain. Learning takes practice and repetition, like any discipline. If your goal is to be the fun teacher, I have news for you: not everybody is going to like you. You want respect.

Expectations of men and women are different in our society. Women are expected to be more nurturing and supportive, and therefore some students may feel more comfortable approaching women for academic favors. In a 2018 study from Eastern Washington University, female professors had to put up with more requests from students for favors like grade increases, deadline extensions, or the opportunity to redo assignments than male professors.

This took an emotional toll on female teachers because students who felt entitled to academic success, regardless of their actual performance, were more likely to a ask a female professor for extra favors and then react negatively if they did not get what they wanted. They were not as likely to nag a male professor after being rejected.

For this reason, female teachers at times feel like they are walking a tight rope: if they are nurturing and supportive, they could risk being perceived as less authoritative and knowledgeable than male teachers. Regardless of your gender, be kind, but set firm boundaries from the start. Expect all students to follow them. As you develop a reputation as a fine teacher, you will be challenged less (Jackson 2019).

When you are part of the team, your colleagues will be more likely to help you when you need help. In the article "15 Ways to Fight Teacher Burnout That Really Work," put out by the blog We Are Teachers, it mentions if you have relationships with your colleagues, you will feel safer asking for help. Chances are these veteran teachers have been through the same issues and can be a wonderful resource. It goes on to say it is bad to pretend everything is wonderful (Adams 2019).

Hopefully, your school has a mentor program for new teachers in your building. At one school, each new teacher was assigned a mentor teacher for the year, and they were required to attend a teacher mentor class for in-service credit once a week during lunchtime for the first few months and then tapered down to once a month. The class was run by a veteran teacher at the school.

Weekly topics included Open House; professional dress and demeanor; student motivation; substitute teachers; office staff; administrative team; the library; fire drills, codes, and other safety procedures; responsibilities of the general education teacher with a student on an IEP; attendance refresher; mental health; school traditions; school counselors; dealing with parents; the credit mill; 504s; perspectives on scheduling; grading practices; late work; point penalties; preparing for and coming back from break; teacher credibility; teaching on a block schedule; and preparing for final exams.

This class is necessary for all teachers new to the building—whether they are new or veteran teachers. Every school is run differently, and to speed up assimilation into the school and to welcome a new teacher, this class is a must. These new teachers can give back later when they are the mentor teacher for a new teacher. It is also a great refresher for veteran teachers. If schools want successful teachers, they must guide and support their new teachers.

The ECO observation is a powerful tool for a school department. ECO means effective classroom observation. It was developed by Cambridge Education. It differs from traditional observations because the observer observes the students and not the teacher. The observer sits in the front of the classroom to watch the students. The focus is on student learning.

The observer answers the questions: How do you know the students are learning? How can you measure learning? The observer also writes down: "Learning was best when . . ."/"Learning could have been better if . . ." A pair of teachers observe each other and provide each other with written feedback at the end of the day. They discuss aloud what they wrote down ("Getting Started with Peer Observation" 2005).

Next the findings are presented during a department meeting. This takes trust, but it brings a department closer and brings consistency to their program. By observing each other, department members are accountable to each other and familiar with what is expected at each level. ECO can result in improved vertical alignment because common end goals can be decided year to year. SLOs (student learning objectives) can be written as a department with a common assessment delineated by what level the student is in.

4

POSITIVE INVESTMENTS MAKE A MEANINGFUL CAREER

You are a model for your students and staff. Be positive. They do look up to you. Be professional in your appearance and your demeanor. Watch what you say at school in the classroom and in the faculty room. What you say reveals more about who you are than the person you are talking about.

Watch negativity and stay clear of negative people. If you have an issue, go directly to the person. Do not talk behind people's backs. If you are that unhappy, transfer to another school. Never bash another teacher and tell parents or students that a previous teacher did not do their job and that is why the student or class is behind. Your job is to take the student or class from where they are and move them forward.

Sign up to help around the school. The more you invest in school, the more you get out of it. Plus, you learn more about your students. It is important you do something new every year to avoid complacency and boredom. Go to events like school plays and football games.

Be an advisor in after-school clubs like the National Honor Society or LGBTQ Plus Club. Consider being the accreditation chair representing your faculty or being a member on the school climate and social committees. Attend concerts, arts nights, and Poetry Out Loud competitions. Judge speech and debate competitions, proctor SAT or ACT college entrance tests, and assist at school fund-raisers.

Be kind to your secretaries, custodians, staff members, and students. You never know when you will need their help. Thank them verbally and write thank you notes when they help you out. When students give you gifts, take the time to send a handwritten note of thanks to their home.

If you have an issue with a student, parent, or staff member, deal with it immediately, professionally, and in person. Start with a positive observation about the person. For example, with a student: "I really appreciate Mark's sense of humor." Then voice your concern in terms of observable behavior, so you are simply providing data and not judging the person. For example, "Susie frequently talks while I am talking or while another student is sharing their answer out loud for the class." Refrain from words like *defiant, rude, hyperactive*, and *disrespectful*, as these are judgment words.

In a 2017 online article by teacher Rebecca Alber, entitled "A Phone Call Home Makes All of the Difference," she cited Harvard education researchers Matthew Kraft and Shaun Dougherty's study on teachers phoning students' homes: "Frequent teacher-family communication immediately increased student engagement. . . . On average, teacher-family communication increased the odds that students completed their homework by 40 percent, decreased instances in which teachers had to redirect students' attention to the task at hand by 25 percent, and increased class participation rates by 15 percent" (Alber 2017).

Next time you call home to mention a student is suddenly not doing their homework, notice if the situation is immediately fixed. Often parents say they really appreciate a teacher's concern, and the student is grateful the teacher cared enough to notice.

The goal of communication is collaboration and not confrontation. You want the person working with you and not against you. At the beginning of a parent-teacher meeting, introduce yourself to the parent by your first and last name to lighten the tension, instead of by your title. Arrange student desks or chairs in a circle before a meeting and never sit behind your desk. You want to get rid of barriers, so the parent does not feel like they are being talked down to. Ask questions to get support from the parent. For example, "What ideas do you have for Susie to listen to others while they are speaking? What has worked at home?"

If the parent gets off topic during a meeting, gently bring them back and remind them of the purpose of the meeting. For example, if a parent says other students blurt out in class and do not get in trouble, remind the parent this meeting is about Susie and how to help her succeed and learn more in class by listening to others.

At the end of the meeting, close the conversation with the next steps and how you will follow up with the parent. If this is a recurring issue, ask the parent to e-mail you every Friday for a while for a weekly report. Do not make more work for yourself and try to remember to e-mail the parent every week. Put the responsibility on them to e-mail you.

Always document all communication with stakeholders including the date, time, person, and content. There are premade communication logbooks available on Amazon, but you can also make your own using a binder and sheet of paper with the above categories. Make multiple copies of the original sheet of paper. Put them in a binder and separate them with dividers by class period. If you communicate with a parent more than once during the school year, you can refer to your previous comments before you contact them.

Call home with good news to build rapport with students and their families. These positive calls can really lift you up after making a series of negative calls. They remind you of all the good going on in the classroom, and parents' responses will validate this (Alber 2017).

Respond respectfully to upsetting e-mails or phone calls from a parent. Forward the communication to your administration so they are in the loop and hear both sides of the story—not just the angered parent's side of the story.

You will be challenged throughout your career, no matter how good a teacher you are. Read the situation below. How would you handle it as a professional teacher?

You are having a great day and it is almost lunch, when an e-mail catches your eye. It reads:

> Dear Mrs. Smith,
> My daughter Susie loved Spanish until this year. You have made her hate Spanish. I know we signed a syllabus agreeing she would turn in all her assignments on time, but you have made her so unhappy, she has not turned in the last 10 assignments. She now has an F in the class. F's are not acceptable in our home. She has never had an F before. I need you to accept all her late assignments for full credit and bring her grade up to an A. I know you will do this because it does not look good for you to have students failing your classes. Please take care of this immediately, or I will take further action.
> Sincerely,
> Mrs. Eileen Jones

What do you do?

1. Ignore the e-mail.
2. E-mail back.
3. Phone her and set up an after-school meeting.

Do not ignore the e-mail! Check your school's policy. In most schools, you must return an e-mail within twenty-four hours or you are at fault.

If you choose to e-mail the parent back, cool down first, then keep it brief and professional. Thank the parent for the e-mail and set up an after-school meeting. Make sure you CC the principal, so the parent can see you are including the administration in any future communications with the parent.

Invite the parent, Susie, and the principal to the meeting. Never hold a meeting without an administrator there. Things could get ugly, and you do not want to be there alone. Do not write anything else in your e-mail. Anything else you write could be held against you by the parent, and you will end up annoying the principal sending them endless trails of all the gory e-mails between you and the parent.

Susie needs to be at the meeting so she can be held accountable. This is Susie's problem that the parent has made their own. Sad to say, but in our world today, some parents cannot separate themselves from their children: they see what happens to their children as a reflection of themselves.

If you do call the parent, thank them for the e-mail and set up a meeting in a calm and professional voice. If the parent tries to go into the details, tell them they will be discussed at the meeting, thank them for the call, and hang up.

If you are unsure how your e-mail or phone call will come across to the parent, have a colleague read your e-mail or rehearse the phone call with you before you communicate with the parent.

Before the meeting, set some goals for yourself. What do you want to accomplish at the meeting? You may want to meet with the principal before the meeting, especially if you are a new teacher, and ask for help in how to run the meeting.

In the book *Becoming*, Michelle Obama said people tend to be more approachable in person, when they see you face to face. If you received a hostile e-mail from a parent, they may be kinder in person.

Remember to stick to the facts in the meeting. If the parent gets into emotional waters, talk less and listen more. Steer the parent back to what is important: the child must take responsibility for their learning—not the parent and not the teacher. You could make a deal: take half the assignments just this time for full credit, but in the future, all assignments must be turned in on time, just like everyone else. Otherwise, this shows favoritism to individual students.

Following the meeting, send a thank you note to the parent thanking them for their support and assistance. Ask them to contact you if there are further concerns. This leaves the door of communication open beyond the meeting.

If the meeting gets out of control, announce the meeting is over and will be rescheduled. Talk with the principal privately afterward and come up with some norms before the next meeting. Announce the norms to the parent at the beginning of the second meeting. Remember to be professional. This is your class, and you are the leader.

Some further communication tips:

1. Avoid reading school e-mails after hours. You need downtime and your sleep. Remember, you are not paid for after hours.
2. Be consistent. If you follow your rules and procedures daily, so will your students. Routines become habits.
3. Be a leader. It is confusing to students if you try to be their friend and then take it personally when they do not follow your rules.
4. Know your school's rules. If you want support from the administration, you must follow the school rules.
5. No matter how good a teacher you are, some parent will challenge you at some point—especially your first years, when parents see you as most vulnerable, and you do not have a reputation as a fine teacher yet.
6. You will be hurt by these e-mails, especially when you care about your job and your students. Talk to a trusted and positive veteran teacher to help you put it into perspective. Most teachers have received nasty e-mails.

In your fifteenth year, you are halfway to retirement—too far along to turn back and too easy to become jaded and complacent. Take the risk and try something new. It could be a change in the grade level you teach, a change in the subject you teach, or even a change in the job you teach within your district. For example, you could retrain to be a guidance counselor after being a teacher. If it does not work out, you will figure out what else to do.

You may have been subconsciously preparing for this move and did not realize it. Maybe you have been attending workshops and institutes in subjects you are interested in. Or maybe you have been doing outside reading in a new direction. You could also go out into your district and observe other teachers teaching at the new level, subject, or job you are interested in. You may be able to remain at your school and do an internal transfer to your new assignment.

Confide in trusted colleagues that you are looking for a new opportunity and see if they know of any openings or have any friends you could observe. Regularly check online job openings in your district. This could be the best decision you ever made. It could give you newfound energy to not only motivate yourself but to further motivate your students. You may be grateful you took the risk.

Stay in touch after your students graduate. The best moments in a teacher's life are when their students return and tell them what they are up to in their life. If you live in a smaller city or town, you may regularly run into your students in the community. It is validation for you that you made a difference in someone's life. As far as online friendships, never let a student befriend you on Facebook while you are their teacher; wait until they graduate from high school.

5

PROACTIVE LEADER: CREATING A POSITIVE CLASSROOM CLIMATE

Proactive is defined as creating a situation by causing something to happen rather than responding to it after it has happened. Believing you are the leader and in charge of your classroom rather than the facilitator can prevent many potential problems. For example, you decide the arrangement, seating, and decor of your classroom. You have the right to change it at any time. Your classroom arrangement determines the flow of the classroom. Your seating determines who you want to sit next to each other. Your decor can demonstrate the passion you have for your subject. If you want student input in these areas, it is at your discretion.

Classroom climate is the prevalent mood and attitudes the teacher and students feel when they are in the classroom. A negative climate can feel hostile or out of control. A positive climate can feel safe and supportive of student learning by both the teacher and other students. Teachers sometimes think they have no control over their classroom climate, that they are stuck with whoever ends up in there. But classroom climate is not predestined; it is created. Classroom rules are important, so students have a predictable, safe learning environment. Only when students feel safe and respected emotionally and physically can they focus better on learning (Kamb 2012).

Teachers need to foster positive peer relationships by deliberately planning relationship activities. Put students in preassigned pairs so no one feels left out looking for a partner. When students can pick their partners, tell any singles to see you immediately and you will match them up.

Teachers need to let their students know they care about them as human beings and not just as students. The first day of school, have students fill out an index card. They write their name, the best way to communicate with them directly (phone or e-mail), the way they learn the best, the way they learn the worst, what interests them in and out of school, and what goals they have in life or at school.

You could even take it one step further: ask students to write on their index card if there is anything else they want to share with you. Some students may want you to know they are shy. Others may want you to know which pronoun to use when you address them. Some may want you to know they have visual or hearing issues and need certain seating accommodations.

When you meet students at the door before class, ask them questions about themselves using the information they wrote down. Use the index cards when randomly calling on students during class, so they do not think you are picking on them individually.

Check on students' perception of classroom climate throughout the year by having them respond to questions in writing like: (1) Do you feel safe in the class? (2) Are students kind to each other in the class? (3) Do students follow the class rules? (4) Do you feel included by the other students? (5) If you answered no to any of the questions, how could the classroom climate be improved?

This perception of classroom climate can be applied to school climate as well, with the same questions addressed to teachers. (1) Do you feel safe at your school? (2) Are other teachers and administrators kind to you? (3) Do teachers follow the school rules? (4) Do you feel included by the other teachers and administrators? (5) If you answered no to any of the questions, how could the school climate be improved? Safety at your school could be interpreted as cleanliness or safety from inside or outside intruders or support from the administration.

You probably remember how you were greeted by the staff when you first entered a school as a new teacher. Teachers and administrators saying they were glad you had come to their school can go a long way to boost your confidence. These words can carry you through tough days because you feel welcome and appreciated. Inclusion makes everyone feel good about themselves, like their opinion matters and is valued.

When staff follow school rules, they are united and strong. When staff do not follow them, resentment sets in and weakness follows to the point that staff gang up on each other either directly or indirectly with a toxic atmosphere resulting.

Administrators can assist staff getting to know each other by putting them in different groups for games, committees, and evaluations of each other. Also, you may get great ideas by observing or speaking with people outside of your department. They may give you fresh insight and solutions to issues from a different perspective.

On the other hand, if administrators never assign their staff to groups and allow them to work with whomever they want, the staff will tend to always work with the same people and some staff may feel left out to the point that they feel unwelcome at the school and that their opinion does not matter.

Carolyn Speer, an education professor at Wichita State University, writes in a May 13, 2017, online article entitled "Establishing Authority in Your Classroom" that "establishing authority is the critical cornerstone to good classroom management, student satisfaction, and student success. . . . It's my opinion that people who are good at running a classroom have a more satisfying career, have students who learn more, and get better teaching evaluations."

Her advice on how to be perceived as being in charge included "you have to believe that authority is legitimate, does not have to be coercive, and will lead to the best outcomes for everyone" (Speer 2017).

John Shindler, a professor of education at California State University in Los Angeles, included the following information on teacher authority in his classroom management resource pages (Shindler 2018). Social psychologists John French and Bertram Raven (1960) identified five basic forms of teacher authority. The five types are: attractive/referent, expert, reward, coercive, and position/legitimate. They believed an effective teacher must incorporate at least some amount of each of these five types of authority. How much of each depended on the teacher's goals and their personality.

The attractive (referent) authority is when the teacher relies on their personality and building relationships with the students. The students perceive the teacher as pleasing, likable, funny, and charming.

Our media-driven culture encourages students to like teachers who are cool. Male teachers have the advantage here—male students like being called "dudes" and having the coach relationship with their teachers. Male students are not receptive to female teachers trying to play this role. Students work harder for teachers they like and perceive as caring. However, if the teacher puts being a friend to the students over being a teacher to them, they may end up giving away their teacher authority and being taken advantage of by the students.

Expert authority is when a teacher is perceived as knowledgeable in their subject and well prepared. This works when students feel there is a lot of value in what their teacher says, and the students want to learn. Also, the teacher is not arrogant and is in tune with the needs of their students. However, some teachers who are passionate about their subjects and not about their students end up leaving the profession because the students are disinterested or disrespectful. Students do not care how much you know until they know how much you care.

Reward authority is when rewards are used to influence student behavior. This could include grades, points, recognition, prizes, praise, privileges, or any other external motivator. But to keep this healthy over time, the teacher needs to help foster intrinsic sources of motivation within the student or the student's only motivation is to obtain the reward rather than learning or growth.

Coercive authority is when the teacher withholds privileges and gives consequences or punishments to students. This means a line has been crossed and something undesirable will happen to the student. All teachers need some amount of coercive authority or some students will likely cross lines since they do not fear consequences. Coercive authority is important to set teacher-student boundaries. This brings security to students who do not cross lines because they know the teacher will step in and act upon the ones who do, so their learning is not disrupted.

However, if this authority is overused, it could result in a hostile classroom climate that undermines class motivation. Shame, punishments, guilt, humiliation, personal attacks, and withdrawal of affection will shut down learning. For example, the strategy of having students call their parents in front of the class when they misbehave could be humiliating to the student, plus learning time is lost. A more effective strategy would be to have the student call their parents immediately after class with only the teacher present.

Position (legitimate) authority is when the teacher has power by default because they are the teacher, the one who is contracted to manage the classroom. Teachers who expect to be given respect usually are, but this takes some confidence and belief in one's abilities. Student teachers, substitute teachers, and new teachers will be tested more if they have not established a reputation at the school as a fine teacher (Shindler 2018).

Student engagement is a buzzword now and most likely written all over your yearly evaluation. Engagement simply means students are on task and doing what they are told to do. But then you say, they are rule followers. Doesn't that stifle creativity and self-expression? No! In fact, you must have rule followers before you can have engagement. Teachers endlessly burn themselves out daily trying to come up with new and exciting ideas to keep 100 percent of their students engaged.

First, it is impossible to keep all students engaged every minute. Second, let me repeat—it is not your job to entertain your students! It is your job to teach. The fun is in the learning. Some days you may have games to apply to previous learning, but some days students are simply learning. Off-task behavior is not engagement and will wear you out as a teacher.

Be the adult and oversee your classroom. If you open yourself up to the students' opinions of everything you do, you will lose your sense of direction and every day will be a fight between you and the students. Newer teachers often say their students do not like them, the textbook, the movies, and the homework in the classroom. Remember these are kids. And they love getting under your skin—if you allow it. Yes, they will say under their breath and just loud enough for you to hear it, "I hate this class."

You may see etched into a desk or a textbook, "I hate . . ." followed by your name. It is upsetting because it is personal; you are giving your best every day, and this is not a token of appreciation. However, try to remember kids can be upset about other factors in their life and take it out on you. Stay focused on your job. This is not a popularity contest. Your goal is for your students to learn.

Student engagement comes after following classroom rules and procedures. The first days of school, you need to lay down classroom rules, consequences, and procedures. Write them into your syllabus, review them daily to reinforce your expectations, put them into practice, and test students (not open book!) on them at the end of the first week. This is not a waste of time: the groundwork you do at the beginning of the year will save you time the rest of the year. Expect students to test the waters. You must be consistent and follow through the rest of the year. When students return from an extended break, that is a great time to review the rules again.

Never get into a negotiating argument with your students. You are the adult. If you find your students are complaining daily about classwork and assignments, you have given up your leadership.

A 1996 online article by Valerie Finholm, a staff writer at *The Hartford Courant*, was entitled, "You're Boss and Don't Let Kids Forget It." She attended a talk by psychologist turned syndicated columnist John Rosemond. He was struggling with his own son's constant behavior problems in elementary school. He and his wife went to parent-teacher conferences and at first blamed the teacher, believing the teacher had a bad attitude toward their son.

Then they realized it was their son not taking any responsibility for his actions. They decided to reject the "nouveau parenting" method taught to college-educated psychologists in the 1960s and 1970s and dispensed to parents because it emphasized the psychological development of the child over character development (Finholm 1996).

Rosemond explained further in a 2016 online article that the new parenting was about properly interpreting and responding to a child's feelings because the old pre-1960s parenting did not allow children to freely express their feelings, and that caused psychological damage. With the new parenting, the child became the center of the family instead of the marriage. One parent said, "I was always striving to be supermom, thinking if I could explain things well enough, my children would accept what I'd said. What I have learned from Dr. Rosemond is my children do not have to be happy all the time. If they are, then I am not doing my job" (Rosemond 2016).

And in fact, in a 2020 online article by Ginna Parsons, Rosemond said research is clear: the more obedient the child, the happier the child. He went on to say the key to getting a child to do as you tell them to do is proper presentation from the adult. Children obey people who look and act confident. So do not get down to the child's level when you talk to them or talk in a pleading voice. Also do not give consequences that mean nothing. The consequence must establish a permanent memory, so the child never wants to repeat the misbehavior again.

Rosemond gave the example of a five-year-old hitting their mother. The mother put the child in a five-minute time-out. He told the mother to prepare for the child to hit her again because the consequence was meaningless. Instead, Rosemond said the child had to go to bed right after dinner every night for one month—no birthday parties, sleepovers, sports, TV time with the family. When the child turned seventy, they would remember being in their room for a month when they were five, and they would never hit their mother again (Parsons 2020).

When the children of new parenting come to school, they have no emotional control. They expect to have their feelings listened to all the time. They expect to be the center of attention, like they are at home, but that is not possible with thirty students in a class. Rosemond says the most relaxed parents are the ones who are the strictest because their children learn early where the boundary lines are drawn. They are not constantly negotiating with their children. This goes for teaching as well.

Once you lay down the law the first week of school, you can go into your classes excited where the content will take you each day, not worrying about if you can even teach it that day (Rosemond 2018; Ross 1998).

The Rosemonds returned to old-fashioned parenting based on the three Rs. The three Rs are respect, responsibility, and resourcefulness. The Rosemonds instituted a strict regime of chores, homework (done with little parental involvement), and discipline. They got rid of the television for four years, as well as most of their children's toys. Three years later, they said their son was "cured." He no longer had discipline issues at home or at school. His schoolwork had also improved. Their son is now a Navy pilot, married, and a father (Parsons 2020).

Watch the tone, volume, and speed of your voice. Leaders speak calmly and do not raise their voices. Leaders speak slower so they are understandable. Leaders do not end a sentence with, "okay?" "Okay" is a suggestion and not an instruction. Leaders do not make statements into questions like, "Can you just finish the paper today?" Instead, they will say kindly but firmly, "Finish the paper today."

Watch your nonverbal cues including facial expressions and eye contact. Make sure you look student(s) directly in the eye(s) when you speak with them. Have a colleague film you. What did you learn from watching yourself?

A middle school band director was teaching her class one day when every time she raised her baton to start a piece (she had taught the students a raised baton meant eyes on her, instruments up in playing position, and silence), one female student would start talking. This was a newer teacher, and she was exasperated with this young lady. She put down her baton and yelled at the female student to "shut up."

This spontaneous unprofessional behavior was embarrassing to the teacher. She vowed never to raise her voice again in her teaching career. In hindsight, she realized she should have taken the student outside of the classroom and calmly taken care of it. If that did not work, she should have called an administrator down. She was humiliated by her reaction, and the class most likely respected her less.

Never punish the entire class for an individual's misbehaviors. Speak immediately with the individual in the hallway outside of the class. Then together with the student, call their parents after class or set up a conference with the parents and student present. At these meetings, be the leader. Speak calmly and listen.

Do not allow students to bully you or make fun of you. Immediately speak with them in the hallway outside of the class. Contact parents, school counselors, and administrators for help, if needed. This also sends a message to the rest of the class that bullying will not be tolerated. How would you handle the following situation as a professional teacher?

You have a student whose parent is a teacher at your school. The student daily walks into class late with their Starbucks coffee, goes to their desk, puts their feet on top of their desk, and announces loudly, "I'm here!"

You speak with their parent—your colleague—and the parent tells you if their child is passing your class academically, the parent does not want to hear about behavioral issues. Now what do you do?

Go to the principal, assistant principal, or dean of students, whoever oversees school-wide student behavior, and set up a conference with them, the student, and yourself. Do not invite the parent, as they have indicated they are not interested in dealing with their child's misbehavior in your class. The administrator needs to tell the student they are not exempt from classroom rules just because their parent teaches at the school. The administrator needs to tell the student that, if there are any more issues, they will be dealing with the student personally.

If the administrator will not back you, the child needs to drop your class because the behavior will only escalate, now that the child knows they have carte blanche to do whatever they want in your classroom.

The toughest parents to deal with can be teacher parents. You must remove your teacher hat when you are a parent in the meeting. This is not your classroom. You are undermining a teacher's authority when you let your child know the class rules do not apply to them. If you feel the teacher's rules are unreasonable, then talk alone with the teacher. Otherwise, respect the classroom rules of your colleagues.

Do not overshare your personal life to get closer to your students. Talking about your personal life is a great way to connect, build rapport with your students, and show you are approachable. If you do not show your human side, students may not connect with you or fear you. However, there is a line between sharing and oversharing.

The National Education Association has four tips for forming better relationships with students:

1. Start simple. Start with small stepping-stones before moving up to more personal topics. For example, you could mention holiday plans to visit family. Little personal snippets show you have a life outside of the classroom that students can relate to without going into deeper detail.
2. Consider their parents. A good rule of thumb is, when sharing details about your personal life, pretend everything you tell your students will be told to their parents. (It probably will be!) If you tell your students, "I am going to meet a friend at a bar," students may tell their parents, "My teacher is going out drinking with friends tonight." This could get you in trouble with parents and administrators.
3. Learn to "code" your activities. Using the example above, instead of saying you are meeting a friend at a bar, you could say, "I am going downtown to see an old friend."
4. Avoid the truly "personal" stuff. Hobbies and interests are fine to share with students, but romantic relationships, family matters, and personal drama are not appropriate to share with your students. Your students may be curious and ask you personal questions, but you have the right to privacy and the right to tell them you will not answer their personal questions. Then change the topic. If a student persists, talk to them privately; tell them they are crossing lines, and you will speak with their parents and the administration if this continues (Sands 2017).

Amy Morin, a psychotherapist, wrote an online article entitled "There is a Clear Line Between Oversharing and Being Authentic—Here's How to Avoid Crossing It." She wrote that because of the invention of reality TV and social media, sharing personal problems has become more socially acceptable than in the past. Some self-help books have encouraged it, saying we need to be more authentic because that makes us more honest and we own our story. What is the difference between being authentic and oversharing? It comes down to intentions.

To be an authentic person, what you say and what you do must line up with your values. In Brené Brown's book, *Daring Greatly* (2012), she wrote, "Using vulnerability is not the same thing as being vulnerable; it's the opposite—it's armor." Why do people cross the line (sometimes unintentionally) from being authentic to oversharing? One reason is a misguided attempt to gain sympathy. If you share your errors to help others learn, you are being authentic. However, if you share those errors to gain pity, you are oversharing.

Another reason people overshare is to fast-track the relationship. Authentic people build relationships over time. Oversharers move quickly to gain a sense of intimacy, without building trust first.

And the third reason for oversharing is your story still owns you. For example, if a person is going through a divorce, they may feel like everyone thinks there is something wrong with them. To ease the anxiety, they reveal their pain. Authentic people accept the anxiety and step back and consider if it is a good idea to share their pain or not.

There can be serious consequences if you overshare. You could put yourself in physical danger by revealing information about yourself to the wrong person. People might become uncomfortable if you share too much with them. Some people could even take advantage of you.

Before you share information with other people, think about why you are doing it and the possible consequences. You can still be an authentic person and maintain your sense of privacy (Morin 2016).

For example, if one of your family members dies, you may feel very raw emotionally. You may wonder if you should tell your students. Some of your colleagues may suggest you tell them, so it takes the pressure off yourself if you are having a bad day emotionally. However, you need time to come to terms with it on your own. You do not want your students responsible for comforting you or feeling sorry for you. You may need to take some time off, so your grief does not affect your teaching.

Go home and grieve with friends and family. Tell your students on a need-to-know basis only; for example, if you are attending the relative's memorial a month later and you will be out of school due to travel out of state. Also, a month later, you could mention it out loud without breaking down.

Some teachers handle grief differently. For some, staying in school and teaching is the comfort of a normal routine to get them through the day before the grief of dealing with relatives in the evening. If you know a colleague is going through a tough time, do not judge them on their actions. Send a nice card to them indicating you care about them and are available if they need help.

Have high expectations for your students and believe they can all learn, and they will rise to the challenge. For example, if you are a world language teacher, you may require full immersion in the target language in your classes. There may be resistance to that. You may receive phone calls from angry parents saying their child should not have to speak in Spanish in your class. You could reply that would be like not requiring a student to play an instrument in music class or dress out for a physical education class.

Convince the parents that if you teach the class methodically and at the appropriate level for their child, the child will be fine. Do not enable your students. They will not be coddled in the real world when they graduate.

Dr. Steven Landfried, a Wisconsin teacher and educational consultant interested in the transition from middle school to high school, wrote an online article in 1990 entitled "Educational Enabling: Is 'Helping' Hurting Our Students?" He gave an example of a student who refused to learn, study for tests, or do assignments because he thought school was supposed to be fun. He knew teachers wanted him to succeed, so he used that as a source of power over them. He would only play the reward-bribe game if the price was right for him. He knew he could not fail because his school employed the "schools without failure" concept.

Teachers and guidance counselors excused his behavior because he was a "troubled kid," and he regularly was excused from class to go to the guidance counselor for help. Maybe the adults had good intentions, but they were teaching the wrong lesson. They were enabling rather than helping this student. Helping makes a child more capable to grow and develop confidence in their abilities especially when there is disappointment or problems arise, while enabling makes them more incapable. Enabling means letting people off the hook and is synonymous with the terms "rescuing" and "coddling."

The word "enabling" has positive and negative connotations. For many years psychologists and educators used it in a positive way. For example, "The intervention of placing Susie in the front row closest to the teacher enabled her to be less distracted from paying attention in class."

However, in the past decade, the word has gotten a negative connotation from drug education programs that use the vocabulary of Alcoholics Anonymous. There "enabling" referred to actions like loaning money to substance abusers or calling in sick for them. There is a term out now called "educational enabling," and this means taking on too many responsibilities for parents and students. Mark Twain once warned, "Never learn to do anything: if you don't learn, you'll always find someone to do it for you." Brutally said, but true.

There are two types of enabling at school: academic enabling and behavioral enabling. Academic enabling is when teachers do not hold students accountable for their academic performance. Here are some examples:

1. not always collecting homework or projects when they are due,
2. allowing students to tune out while the teacher does the talking and thinking,
3. accepting late assignments or accepting them without penalty,
4. giving credit for sloppy work,
5. ignoring cheating or giving a mild consequence for it,
6. giving easy tests and grades that require little or no studying,
7. allowing students who have not studied or turned in work most of the semester to pass with extra credit work, and
8. backing off on assigning homework because most students are not doing it.

Behavioral enabling is when teachers reinforce self-indulgence, bad attitudes, and disrespect for self and others when they accept irresponsible or unacceptable behaviors from individual students or entire classes.

Examples of behavioral enabling are:

1. allowing students to sleep, read newspapers, or carry-on irrelevant conversations with other students during class activities;

2. making excuses for students ("He didn't mean to hit him; there was a full moon out.");
3. accepting flimsy excuses from "good students" for inappropriate behaviors that would not be accepted from "troublemakers";
4. repeating questions for students not paying attention; and
5. picking up trash for students or cleaning graffiti off desks (Ginsburg 2011; Landfried 1990).

Guidance counselors can also enable students. They might:

1. knowingly accept lies from parents who call to excuse student absences or
2. let students switch out of classes just because the child says they have a personality conflict with the teacher when the student resents the teacher for expressing and enforcing clear expectations and that the student must put in effort for their grades.

Administrators enable students when:

1. they ignore academic or behavioral violations because the individual student is needed for athletic or academic competitions or they are in a band concert or a school play;
2. they allow regularly "forgetful" students out of class to call parents to bring lunches, books, or assignments to school;
3. they ask custodians to clean up messes in hallways or classrooms rather than insisting the violators do it;
4. they gloss over profanity, racial and ethnic slurs, or fights to avoid hassles with students and parents; and
5. they support the parents over the teacher because they want peace, and it gets the parents off their back.

Parents enable students when:

1. they regularly fight their battles for them;
2. they lie and call in excused absences and tardiness for them; and
3. they say, "My kid would never do that," "I think you must have misinterpreted what happened," "I think you have a personality conflict with my child," or "My child tells me that so and so started

it," and make it the educator's fault, without listening to their side of the story.

Landfried (1989) wrote, "Allowing students to be lazy or irresponsible exacts a major price from our society. The growing inefficiency and declining productivity of our workers and our declining capacity to compete effectively in the international market, the rising cost of remedial programs to train high school dropouts, teenage parents, and skill-deficient adult workers, the perpetuation of the welfare state mentality—could these conditions exist in part because schools, parents, and society are enabling young people to become less than they can be?"

The person in the end who suffers the most from the enabling is the student themselves. They fall apart when they need to take on grown-up responsibilities like family, professional, and financial obligations, and there is no safety net to catch them. Their boss will not tolerate their coming to work late, their creditors will not tolerate late payments, and their spouse will not tolerate excuses for not doing chores around the house or taking care of the children.

Most educators go into the field because they want to help their students learn. However, some go too far and do things for students that the students really should be doing for themselves because these educators like feeling needed. They avoid hassles from students, parents, and the administration because they are "the nice person." They tell themselves they are the savior because the student just needs love and the other teachers do not understand the student.

The development of codependency leads the student to expect the teacher to rescue them, and that reinforces the teacher's view of being the savior. What these educators fail to see is enabling these students can be harmful to them in the long run. These students, instead of gaining confidence in themselves and their abilities, lose self-esteem and believe they are not capable of improving themselves.

Educators need to look at themselves and figure out why they need to feel needed. What are they getting out of this? Does being liked by others make them feel better about themselves at the expense of helping the student grow up? (Landfried 1990, 12–15).

To reduce enabling, Landfried writes,

1. Realize that good teachers do not give a good education to students: they provide experiences that facilitate and motivate youngsters to educate themselves through trial and error, success, and failure.
2. Develop in-service training to help staff learn to distinguish between helping and enabling behaviors because students cannot shirk academic and social responsibilities inside or outside of the classroom if adults do not enable them. Educators need to model that significant learning and personal growth can only come from hard work and perseverance. Educators need to model the classroom and life importance of organization, persistence, dependability, and punctuality.
3. Teachers need to learn to live with silence when students do not answer their question immediately and not jump in to fill in the answer for them or accept "I do not know" for an answer. Teachers need to expect and encourage students to come up with their own answers.
4. Educators need to talk directly with students about the difference between helping and enabling and why it is important students are not enabled.
5. Educators need to develop the courage to stand up to students and parents who try to pressure them to accept less than the personal best from each student.
6. Students need to feel the consequences of success and failure and, therefore, the self-satisfaction of learning they can overcome adversity, meet challenges, and even accept defeat in cases where one gives everything. When students respect themselves, they can respect others around them and be more empathetic to the struggles their classmates are going through (Landfried 1989).

Tracy Gerhardt-Cooper, a veteran English teacher and parent, wrote a 2019 online article entitled "Empowering Kids Will Take Them Further Than Enabling." She mentioned one of the best things parents can do to empower their children is to teach them to advocate for themselves.

Parents need to teach their children how to approach their teachers in person and via e-mail because this is a communication skill they will need when they enter college and the workforce. The child can contact the teacher when they will be away on an upcoming vacation, when they need assignments that they missed in class if they were sick, or when they need help with a concept taught in class.

Parents can also teach their child time management because honoring deadlines and class start times is a basic skill for becoming a successful college student and effective employee. Gerhardt-Cooper gave the example: "Instead of stopping at Dunkin' Donuts before dropping the kids off, insist they are ready early if they want to make that stop before school. The number of students who stroll in late with steaming coffee and fresh pastries is astonishing. Enabling lateness is a disservice to them" (Gerhardt-Cooper 2019).

One time a high school administration, in a plea to stop excessive tardiness, pulled the guilty students without warning out of attending a special spirit assembly as punishment. Instead, they had to go to the library, work on homework, and speak with several teachers about why they were habitually tardy.

An administrator welcomed them to the library and explained why they were there. A few of the students yelled at the administrator and said their rights were violated and they threatened to get up and leave. The administrator said nothing but called in school police to keep them there.

One teacher sat down next to a senior and asked them to tell them their story. This student was late almost every day to their first period class because they knew the teacher would go over with them at lunch whatever they missed that day, so there was no reason to get up early for their first period class. The teacher asked the student if they realized the teacher was giving up their lunch for them. They told the student lunchtime was not part of the teacher's contract. The student said they had never thought of that because the teacher never complained about it.

The teacher asked the student to put themselves in this teacher's shoes—that they had no break all day. The teacher also told the student if they were regularly late to a future job, they would be fired, and high school was a training time for the future. The student replied they would never be late to the class again. The teacher told the student they would check with them daily to make sure they were following through. They were never late to that class again.

Gerhardt-Cooper wrote that parents also need to teach their children the power of humility. Parents need to model for children how to apologize and admit their wrongs. She said, "When children accept responsibility, demonstrate humility, and learn to make things right, they are exponentially more coachable, teachable, and employable."

Teachers can model this for their students when they apologize for an error and accept responsibility for it. For example, if a teacher is unfair to a student, they can apologize directly to them and ask for their forgiveness. This shows the teacher humbly owns up to their mistake and wants to make things right to reestablish their connection with their student (Gerhardt-Cooper 2019).

When a student sincerely apologizes to a teacher and wants to rectify the situation, this is an opportunity to clean the slate—a chance to start over together again in good faith.

Gerhardt-Cooper writes that students mess up sometimes and that is okay. Allow the natural consequences of failure to happen. For example, if a student fails a test because they did not study, they have learned to associate cause with effect. If they get zeroes on homework for not doing it, or if they get a lower grade for turning it in late, they have learned to associate cause with effect.

These results will not kill them. They may teach them a lesson about priorities and time management. They will not learn this if they are given multiple chances to retake a test or opportunities to make up homework with no consequences. School is low stakes as compared to the real world: if an employee is irresponsible, they could be put on probation or fired.

Gerhardt-Cooper writes that parents need consequences at home as well. She has noticed students failing classes or spending lots of time in the discipline office, yet they still have car keys and cell phones in their hands.

She mentions there are exceptions when the parent does have to take the lead. Perhaps a teacher has been unreasonable, or a situation is beyond what a child can handle alone. Then a parent does need to step in, but not on a regular basis (Gerhardt-Cooper 2019).

Before a parent steps in, they might want to talk with their child, so the child has some input and does not feel the parent is talking behind their back. For example, a child receives an 89.9 percent in a high school English class, and the child knows it will be a "B" because his teacher has stated in their syllabus they do not round up grades. The parent asks the child if it is okay if they speak with their teacher. The child says no because they cut it too close and it is their fault. The child accepts responsibility and takes ownership of the situation.

Or the student in the same situation above requests the parent talk with the teacher because they think the "B" is unreasonable. The parent now must decide how to handle this. They may tell their child the child must handle it themselves and go directly to the teacher. If the parent steps in, they must consider if this is enabling or helping their child and why they are stepping in.

There are exceptions where the parent may need to go behind the child's back and talk with the teacher and administration if they feel the child's safety is in jeopardy and the child does not want the parent to speak with the school officials.

If you have students and their parents try to negotiate their grades with you, and you feel their grade was arrived at fairly, stand your ground and tell them the next time they need to work harder if they want a better grade. Make the students responsible.

Have boundaries. Separate your home life from your professional life. At home, focus on taking care of you and your family. Do not read school e-mails. Do not have your schoolbag in your bedroom. At school, have specific days and times for office hours, for example, Tuesdays and Thursdays from 2:30 to 3:15. Write this in your syllabus and post it outside of your door, along with your class schedule. Write in your syllabus that office hours are for students who are keeping up with their work. It is not your job to help students who ignore you in class and take no responsibility for turning their work in.

If a student shows up beyond your office hours and you are still at school preparing your lessons, it is not your responsibility to stop and help them. Repeat your office hours to this student and tell them they need to return during those times. If a parent tells you they want to drop their kids off at 6:30 a.m. on their way to their job to get extra help from you and those are not your office hours, tell them that will not work. Tell them your office hours.

If the parent argues they know you are at school anyway, tell the parent this is your teacher preparation time. Do not give this time away. This is your time to set up and calm down before the rush begins.

Try to avoid lunchtime as your office hours, as you need the downtime, unless you prefer this time. Lock your door at lunchtime and ignore the knocking. It will stop if you do not continuously open the door.

Have students sign up in a binder for office hours with a limit to how many can come at a time. Another reason to have them sign up in a binder is to cover yourself: if a parent complains in a meeting their child never got extra help from you, mention your office hours and have a record they never signed up for help. Students need to come by themselves and not bring their friends, as this is not a social hour.

Tell students coming to office hours to bring homework from other classes and work on it quietly as you go around and help individual students. Remember, you are their teacher and not their tutor. If students need more time and individual focus than your office hours can provide, refer them to a tutor.

Teachers by nature are givers and some of the burnout they bring upon themselves because they are afraid or uncomfortable setting boundaries. Other professions set boundaries. Doctors are not available 24-7 including lunchtime to parents and their children. Yet signs have been seen in newer teachers' rooms saying to e-mail them at any time for anything. Is that in the students' best interest? Does this create codependent students?

If a parent says they are upset because you will not give up your lunchtime to tutor their child, who is heavily involved in sports and extracurricular activities and unable to make regular after-school office hours, tell them lunchtime is your teacher collaboration time. The parent and child are making the choice to put extra activities before curriculum. They could talk to the coach and come later to practice sometimes.

Lunchtime is your time to recharge so you are reenergized for your afternoon classes. Whether you spend it with other teachers or alone in your room with the lights off and soft classical music playing, it is your gift to yourself and to your students.

If you are having a rough day at school, look for the positives. Notice the students who are following your rules and procedures and thank them. Seek support from mentors if needed. Sometimes you may exaggerate in your mind how bad a day is.

Keep a journal and write in observable terms what happened that day. Be specific. For example, "Three students, Katie, Travis, and Sarah, were throwing paper airplanes around the room." This will detach you from the situation and help you come up with strategies to prevent this. Also, it will make you realize it was not the entire class. If you have a good day, write down what happened in observational terms. For example, twenty-eight of your thirty students raised their hands to provide input instead of blurting out their answers.

Have a mantra from day one. For example, "Every child has the right to learn." Do not tolerate any student distracting another student from learning. That includes put-downs and bullying. If you move a student's seat at any point and they ask you why, repeat your mantra.

Keep your classroom spending low. Do not buy prizes for every game you play in class. Keep track of the winners of every game, and at the end of the year, award the top three scorers in every class.

Extra credit must always be offered to the entire class and never individually, or it shows favoritism.

Mix it up to keep you and your students interested. Some days will be lecture information standards-based days. Other days will be activity days to apply the knowledge. What you teach may be dictated, but how you teach it is up to you. One time a student mentioned they noticed the shorter the list of required steps for the day written on the board, the more fun the day would be.

6

PATIENCE AND HUMOR IN THE CLASSROOM

Anything worth teaching must be repeated. Do not expect your students to get concepts the first time. Guide your students, have them practice, and then have them apply the concept one step further. Continue to review the concept in daily review sponges at the beginning of classes.

Be careful of jumping to conclusions. If a student arrives tardy to class every day, instead of yelling at them, ask them why. Maybe they are babysitting their younger siblings until their mom comes home after working the night shift. Call their mother and tell her you are concerned they are missing out on learning. Perhaps a neighbor, who also has a child at the school, could drop both children off in the morning.

Having a sense of humor can deflect a situation and save face for a child. If a student is being hard on themselves for not understanding a concept after repeated explanations from you, find a lighthearted way to privately convey to the child they are fine, everyone has tough obstacles at some point in their life, and they will get through this. Just make sure the humor is with them and not at them, like a putdown. For example, "Johnny, let's let the snow fall and try again tomorrow."

In some types of classes, it may be more difficult to show a sense of humor. For example, if you have sixty students in a band class, if you stop to say something amusing, it might be harder to get the class back on track. Use your judgment. But do think about humor: are you avoiding using it in class because you equate being serious with being in control of the class, and thus better learning for the students?

Could there be a balance in your use of humor—be a bit more playful in your teaching yet still oversee your classes? Will the use of humor better connect you with your students? Are you afraid to be funny because you might be vulnerable to your students? Are you afraid of revealing yourself in unrehearsed moments? Are you afraid you do not have a sense of humor?

How do you insert your humorous side into your teaching? Maybe you do not know where to begin. You know you want to be yourself and your humor to be appropriate. You still want to be a model for your students, so you do not want to say anything demeaning, disrespectful, or sarcastic.

One day, now that you are thinking about humor, it may happen by accident. For example, you are demonstrating the skits the students will be working on in small groups. You change your voice to play different characters and really get into telling the story with emotional expressions and actions. The students are laughing with you, and you hear yourself laugh.

You have never heard yourself laugh during a class before. It is so liberating and so human! It also gives the students permission to be funny in their skits. Your high school evaluator notices and writes in your evaluation that one of your strengths is your sense of humor. Who knew? And you always thought you were such a serious person. What a compliment! But best of all, it has helped your students learn and motivated them in your classes (Stanley 2017).

In an online article by university teachers Clio Stearns and Lesley Chapel entitled "Using Humor in the Classroom," they mention laughter as a genuine and authentic human reaction to something funny. Laughter is excitement, and feeling excited is an important part of curiosity, one of the most significant aspects of learning. Humor keeps students engaged, interested, and part of the classroom community and keeps things in perspective when the content feels difficult. Humor also shows your students you are humble if you can laugh at yourself when you make a mistake (Stearns and Chapel n.d.).

A 2017 online article by Florida professors Alissa Klein and Christian Moriarty entitled "You're Funnier than You Think: Using Humor in the Classroom" identifies two different approaches to infusing humor into the classroom. The first is: be funny yourself. This first approach is more challenging and not something everyone can do if it does not come naturally to them. The second approach is: bring in humorous content from other sources. Bring in funny video clips or images. This approach can also be used for online classes. You could even have humorous instructions on a test or funny character names in test questions. Of course, teachers are not funny all the time, or it would lose its effect, and humor is but one classroom tool. You are not an entertainer, but using humor can help with student attentiveness, anxiety reduction, participation, and information retention (Klein and Moriarty 2017).

Another thing that may be hard for teachers besides being funny is singing with their classes. Choral teachers will find this more natural because they are trained to sing with their classes.

Instrumental music teachers or nonmusic teachers may have to work at singing with their classes, especially if they think they have a terrible singing voice. An instrumental music teacher once described taking a required vocal technique class where they had to sing a solo for the final exam. They said it was the most frightening class they ever took, and when they heard themselves sing the solo, it felt like an out-of-body experience to hear themselves sing. They could not relate that sound to themselves.

Start singing privately at home first to your dog or cat or in the shower. Record yourself and get used to your own voice! Sing with trusted friends just for fun. Pretend it is normal for you until it becomes normal for you. No excuses about your singing voice. Be proud of your singing voice. The goal is to enjoy singing and not worry about being perfect.

Once you accept your singing, now start using singing as a participatory activity in your classes instead of a passive listening activity. Expect your students to be resistant at first. But once they see it is no big deal to you, they will sing aloud with you in your classes. This is amazing because society does not encourage singing out loud. It is okay to listen, but singing out loud is embarrassing.

The next time the national anthem is sung at a baseball game or Christmas carols are sung at church, look around. People are mouthing the words, but most are not singing out loud. Singing out loud is another varietal option for your teacher tool kit. One of the best things you can do for world language classes is sing with your students because singing improves pronunciation, introduces new vocabulary, and teaches them songs important to other cultures. Challenge students to write songs in their target language using familiar childhood tunes and gestures to act out a recipe using commands and food vocabulary.

But singing is not just for world language classes. Use your creativity and try it in other classes like history to learn songs associated with historical events or math class to memorize formulas. The sky is the limit!

Part II

Creating Success Outside of the Classroom

7

PRESENT FOR YOU FIRST AND THEN FOR OTHERS

How do you start your morning before school? This is especially important. It can totally color your day and the relationship with your students. Create a ritual because it will provide comfort, structure, and me time for you.

Yoga implements some great self-awareness strategies. Upon awakening, find a quiet place in your home and sit or lay down. Check in with yourself. How are you feeling today physically, emotionally, and spiritually? Label it in your mind. That can diffuse negative feelings, so they do not overwhelm you because you accept yourself where you are at that day. Now take in five deep breaths through your nose and exhale deeply through your open mouth. Take in joy, kindness, good health, gratefulness, love, confidence, and so on. Exhale stress, sadness, anger, fear, disappointment, doubt, and other negative feelings.

As you proceed to your shower or bath, in your mind, describe the steps. For example, "I am opening the door of the shower; I am turning on the faucet for the shower head; I am waiting for the water to get hot before I step into the shower." Continue with brushing teeth, getting dressed, and so forth. This will put you in the present instead of thinking about the past or the future. Notice if you feel calmer now. Notice if this carries over into the classroom. Remember to always take care of yourself first because once you get to school, you are focused on taking care of others.

When you are fully present in the classroom, it might feel like you are in the zone instead of rushing through your lesson. Interestingly, you will get through the lesson whether you feel rushed or calm. It just may take a little longer.

Anxiety is something not commonly talked about among teachers. It requires letting down your guard and being comfortable enough to share it with a trusted colleague. It requires not shaming yourself. A 2017 survey by the American Federation of Teachers confirmed teacher anxiety is higher than most other professions. Sixty-one percent of educators reported their work was always or often stressful. This is twice the rate of other professions.

"Teacher Depression and Anxiety Are So Common," by Jennifer Fink, is a superb article on managing teacher depression and anxiety. She suggests that you buddy up with another teacher, seek professional help, exercise, find an activity or hobby that interests you to remind you who you are outside of a teacher, go out with friends, establish routines and boundaries, take a mental health day occasionally, or change schools to a more supportive environment (Fink 2018).

For example, in the category of establishing routines, have a set time to grade papers daily and stick to it. That may keep you more efficient because you are aware of a deadline and you need to figure out before you begin how you will finish by that deadline.

Become aware of your own anxiety by keeping a diary. For example, you notice regular moderate anxiety when there is a break from school such as on Sunday evenings or after an extended school vacation. You deal with it by putting Monday's lessons on the board every Friday afternoon before you leave school or by going into school before a vacation ends for an hour to put your lessons on the board. During the week, you put the next day's lessons on the board before you leave school. Then you can completely disengage from your job and enjoy your time off.

You may have a stretch with severe anxiety and have no idea where it came from or why. For example, a teacher suddenly has the physical symptoms of being out of breath and grabbing onto their podium to keep them upright. They feel out of control. They look at the students' baskets underneath their desks and wish they could crawl into them.

Their voice may sound outwardly the same, and they may be unsure if the students notice it or not, but they do not feel present. They are fighting their inner self. They do not tell anyone because they feel very ashamed. They hope the anxiety will just disappear.

What finally shuts down the anxiety a week later is when they realize the students were not causing the anxiety, but they were bringing it on themselves. They have the control to pull themselves out of it.

However, sometimes teachers cannot pull themselves out of it. It is like they are drowning without a lifejacket to save them. If you cannot get out of anxiety on your own, seek professional help. This is a form of self-care: to realize a situation is beyond you and you need outside help.

8

PREPARED AND NOT FRAZZLED

Do as much as you can the night before, so you are not frazzled and late to work. Have a specific place for keys, coat, cell phone, and so forth. It is not fair to be yelling at your spouse, kids, and pets when you misplace items. Then everyone has a bad start to their day. Make a healthy lunch for yourself instead of running to an off-campus restaurant. This will save you money and time. A healthy lunch and snacks will give you good energy throughout the day.

Always carry a water bottle with you. Dehydration does affect your mood and cognitive processes. Teachers need to stay positive and think clearly. Healthline recommends you drink half a gallon of water per day, or eight eight-ounce glasses. Many teachers have plenty of water but do not take the time to drink it. Drink a whole glass of water at the beginning of the day, during break time, at lunch, and after school. Make it a habit, so you do it automatically.

Teachers do not drink water sometimes because they feel they do not have enough time to go to the bathroom. Take care of yourself and take the time to go to the bathroom. Go in between classes and lock your door so students are not in your room unsupervised. If you have an urgent situation and you have to use the bathroom during class, leave your door open and arrange with the teacher next door to keep an eye on your students.

Have cough drops and a water bottle on your desk in case of a dry throat. Have a mini refrigerator for perishable food and a mini microwave to warm your food in your classroom if your school allows it. If not, store your food in the faculty room refrigerator.

Make sleep a priority. Loss of sleep makes it harder to think, harms your health, and is hurtful to your mood.

Get plenty of exercise. Give to yourself so you can give to others. During the school day, take an outside walk during lunch alone or with colleagues to reset for the afternoon.

Make time for meditation at home to still your mind. Meditation can also be done at school during lunch or your prep period.

Keep your professional and private life separated as much as possible. Be present 100 percent for each one of them. Stay after school on Friday to finish grading papers, put Monday's plans on the board and Monday's handouts on the front table, and then go home and do not think about school until Monday morning. If you take work home with you on the weekend, it will be like you never left school. You may feel resentful. If you feel resentful, stop and acknowledge it, and try to figure out why you feel this way.

If you sometimes feel resentful when students stay home sick or are absent for family vacations during school days, maybe you need a day off. It is okay to take a mental health day occasionally because you will be a better teacher when you return. Do not announce to the students that you are taking a mental health day. Do tell them at the beginning of the year your rules and expectations when a substitute is in the room. If the students ask where you were, tell them you had an appointment and then change the subject. After all, you did have an appointment with yourself.

Another benefit to finishing your work Friday after school and not taking work home with you on the weekend is that you are not stressed on Sundays worrying about the next week. You are all set to go and are looking forward to returning to an organized classroom with a new spirit of energy for the week.

9

PART OF THE TEAM: KNOWING YOUR COLLEAGUES OUTSIDE OF SCHOOL

Do go to faculty social events outside of school. Get to know your colleagues as people. You never know when you will need their help. They will be more apt to help you if they know you. If you are an introvert and do not feel comfortable at parties, ask people to tell you about themselves. People appreciate others who listen to them.

Being on the social committee at your school is a great place to mix with your colleagues. It is fun to plan yearlong activities for your staff to build cohesion and keep them upbeat. Sometimes administrators are members of this committee also, so this is a great chance to get to know them outside of school and build rapport with them. Make sure your committee welcomes school secretaries and custodians, as they are part of the staff also.

For example, you could help plan the annual murder mystery and dinner. It could be held in early spring when the weather is cold and gray and the days need a bright spot. The committee could buy a murder mystery kit and copy the script and character descriptions multiple times.

The committee could share the character descriptions with the staff via their mailboxes or e-mail or at the end of a staff meeting. Staff could look over the character descriptions and choose the character they want to portray. They could sign up on a list with their name and character choice. (If there are twenty characters and you have a larger faculty, you might have multiple people sign up to play the same character.)

Plan to meet outside of school at a local restaurant that has arranged a separate room for the group. Have staff come dressed as their character. Meet in the lounge first and take pictures of each other in costume. Post those photos in the faculty lounge later.

Have the committee preassign seats at the tables. Hand the staff scripts that indicate when for example, Sarah 1 speaks and when Sarah 2 speaks. Have faculty stand and read their part aloud when it is their turn so everyone can hear them. Eat dinner and read between the bread and butter, appetizer, salad, soup, main dish, and dessert courses. This could take several hours. If it is successful, staff will go home in great spirits and talk about it for weeks afterward at school.

10

POSITIVE: AN IDENTITY OUTSIDE OF SCHOOL

Have a support system of close friends and family who will not judge you.

Have an identity outside of school and outside of the home. Value that identity and nurture it. You matter.

In your early years of teaching, you might get married or be single and have small children. You may notice you are exhausted between the demands of teaching and being a parent. It is like having two full-time jobs. How can you reenergize yourself when you feel depleted?

Schedule time to go to the gym before school or right after school. Put your kids in an after-school program at their school, so you can exercise for an hour several days a week. Find an exercise activity that you enjoy. You could go on the elliptical and read a book or watch a TV program. You could join a Pilates class. You could swim laps in a pool. The regular break will make you a better parent and teacher.

As far as paying for child care, it can be costly, but there are ways to get around it. You could watch a parent's kids several days a week and then they watch your kids, so each of you can get a break. Do not use money as an excuse to not take care of yourself.

If you are single, it is vital your life is beyond school and your home. You may not have children to tend to, but you also need a break from teaching. Remember: whatever interests you pursue make you a more interesting person—and thus a more interesting teacher.

Continue your hobbies that bring you joy. Keep singing in your local choir. Watch the energy surge back into you. Watch how you have more energy for teaching and more patience with your own children. Your colleagues may be amazed at how you manage all of this. You can reply that you find time for things that matter to you.

Or perhaps you will buy gym equipment for your home. Just make sure you set a regular exercise time and instruct your family not to disturb you unless it is an emergency. You could even tell your family that you must work out regularly or you will get sick. After all, that is the truth. Do what is best for you. For some teachers, a separate gym works better because it is a clear separation from their responsibilities: a regular time just for them. This is not selfish—it is necessary.

When you make time for things that matter to you, it is easier to keep things in perspective and not take them personally: If you have a bad day at school, it does not mean you are a bad person.

11

PROACTIVE LEADER: STANDING UP FOR YOUR TEACHER RIGHTS

Of course you always want to anticipate situations so you can prevent them as much as possible. But there are times when you must stand up for yourself when you feel you have been wronged. It is a form of self-care because it demonstrates you believe in yourself. It would be easier to have other teachers stand with you, but if they will not for fear of their own job security, or they cannot, then you must stand alone. The following are examples of standing up for yourself in your teaching career. This may be very painful, but it will make you a stronger person and teacher.

Grades are important to teachers, parents, and their children. Grades for parents and their children are an entrance indicator into college. Grades for the teacher indicate a student values learning, self-discipline, and a work ethic to understand and apply the material presented in class.

Nowadays grades are an up-to-the moment event posted online and available immediately. Often, once a child reaches high school, parents want their child to be responsible for their own grades, and parents want to free themselves from grade responsibility.

How much freedom is best? It depends on the child. Is the child taking responsibility for their learning? Notice this is not about grades. Evidence: the child comes home and regularly studies and does homework = less monitoring. The child comes home and sometimes studies and does homework = more monitoring. The child comes home and never studies nor does homework = a lot of monitoring.

It is important the student makes the connection between effort and knowledge learned. This does not always result in better grades. The goal is for the parent not to focus solely on results (grades), so they model that the process and the integrity of getting there is more important than the results. The goal is for the student to value the learning process.

A situation: you have an upset student who sees you after class because they have a D in high school math. They tell you they are not good at math. You ask them how much they study, go to office hours, and turn in assignments. They admit they are not studying, not coming to office hours, and not turning in assignments on a regular basis. They assume everyone in the class is smarter than they are.

When you tell the student their classmates are not smarter than they are but put in the effort, the student begins studying, coming to office hours, and turning in all their assignments. At the end of the year, you receive a thank you note from them. They say you taught them a life lesson that you must put in the effort to learn. They had always coasted effortlessly through their classes in middle school and did not see the connection. They write that their grades have improved in all their classes.

Before the mid-1990s, teachers still had a syllabus that indicated the percent of grading with categories such as tests and quizzes, but the difference was, they did not have computers. A child's grade was calculated by hand by the teacher at the end of the quarter and semester. Students did not know their grades until they received their report card.

Now teachers enter grades online in live time. Students and parents have access to those grades literally seconds after they are entered. Students and parents could e-mail you immediately after a grade is entered to contest a grade. It is important to respond within twenty-four hours with your answer. It is important to double-check a grade. Teachers make mistakes.

When parents contact you about a grade, they are usually at wit's end. They want a quick solution. They are focused on the grade (result) and not the learning process. They do not want their child or themselves held accountable, so they blame the teacher. There is a balance issue. Ideally, the teacher teaches, the parent parents, and the student learns. The parent feels the teacher has not done a good job teaching. Generally, parents do not monitor their child at the appropriate level until there is a disaster: the child has an F in the class.

But what if your answer does not satisfy them? Teachers have had property damaged in retaliation: cars broken into in their driveways, tires slashed, items stolen out of their cars. If possible, do not live near your school, to avoid students following you home. Do not leave valuables in your car. Park your car in your garage and not in the driveway at night.

If a parent is not satisfied with your grade explanation for their child, they may go to an administrator at your school to complain and demand a grade change. Even after you show the evidence how the student acquired that grade, they may still threaten to go to the superintendent of schools if you do not change the grade. Now what do you do?

After asking the parents to wait outside, the administrator may tell you they will support you either way—standing your ground or giving in to their demands. If you stand your ground, you will most likely win in the end, but at what price to you? You will lose sleep over it, be dragged through the mud, and in the end be put through unbelievable stress. This is a very tough decision that only you can make. There are times to fight it and times to let go and move on.

Do not let yourself be overscheduled. If you have a supervisor schedule you to teach ten elementary music classes in a row in one day moving between three schools, that is too much. You barely make it to each school on time. You ask him when you are supposed to eat lunch, and he responds, "In your car." You ask him when you are supposed to go to the bathroom, and he responds, "Bring a toilet into your classroom." Do consider joining the teachers' union. Go to the teachers' union. They can negotiate for a break for you. They may even have your supervisor teach the class you are excused from teaching, so you have a break in your day.

Amanda Coffman, a Kansas City middle school teacher, resigned in front of the school board on February 10, 2020, when the Shawnee Mission School District failed to successfully negotiate with the teachers' union and imposed a three-year unilateral contract. The district told the teachers to accept the new contract and continue working under the 2019 contract or resign. Coffman chose to resign.

She told her students to watch the live broadcast ahead of time as she addressed the students directly. She said, "You all know that the most important lesson I want you to take away from your time with me is just because you can, does not mean you should. . . . I could accept this contract, smile and stay silent about the lies the district perpetuates about its teachers, but that does not mean I should."

The negotiations centered on how the district would spend $9.6 million in restored state funding. The union asked the district to properly compensate teachers and ease their workloads since many of the teachers were working six classes out of seven periods, one more period than their neighboring districts. The district argued hiring seventy additional teachers to address workload concerns would cost the district $5 million, money the district said it did not have (Chan 2020).

On February 14, 2020, the Kansas Department of Labor sided with the teachers' union over the school district. They said the district committed a "prohibited labor practice" when it imposed a three-year unilateral contract on the teachers. The ruling invalidated the second and third year of this contract. The department decided the district did not have the authority to issue such a long-term contract, saying it was denying the union its right to negotiate terms for the coming school years. The district is appealing this decision. A federal mediator stepped in to decide on a contract for this year, which was agreed upon in March.

As for Amanda Coffman, she still does not regret that she stepped down because "the same people who would seek to do something that was found to be illegal are still in charge. I am very hopeful the negotiating team is able to be more successful next year, and things improve for teachers in Shawnee Mission, but I am not willing to wait any longer for that to happen."

Coffman says she will probably eventually to return to teaching. In the meantime, she has had to face criticism from Internet users over her broadcast resignation gone viral. She said, "Internet fame, which many of you crave, is hollow. . . . One million people think they know exactly one thing about me. And they all have strong opinions about that one thing. Write your life like you would a good story. Be a round, full character in your future. I am more than the day I quit. You are more than your favorite video game" (Moxley 2020; Dempsey 2020).

Ask for help and clarification when you need it. If an administrator sends via e-mail a long list of evaluation demands to the faculty and no one understands but tries to comply, yet the faculty keeps getting written feedback that they are not doing it correctly, it is time to speak up.

Politely tell the administrator everyone is at an impasse and cannot complete the list without their help. The administrator will appreciate this because they do not want an unhappy faculty. The administrator could discuss this in a faculty meeting or come down to your room and explain it very thoroughly. You could turn around and explain it to your department and other departments as well. It is a win-win situation for everyone.

Fight for your rights when you feel your life is in danger. If you receive an anonymous death threat in your school mailbox or via e-mail that says something like, "I know where you live, and I am going to come over to your house and murder you and your family," it is time to act. Do not view this as a baseless prank or feel silly going to your administrator. You have been threatened.

Bring the note to your administrator, and if you think you know who wrote it, tell them their name. If your administrator tells you this is a tricky situation because they do not want to accuse a child of something no one witnessed—a counselor would have to talk with the child and even then, if the child denied it, they could not directly accuse the child—then you must stand firm.

This is not a matter of saving face for the child or keeping them in your class until the issue is resolved. This is your life. Tell the administrator the child must be removed from your class immediately because you are unable to teach the class thinking they could bring a gun to school at any point and endanger your life as well as their fellow classmates.

Tell the administrator you will give them this student's homework and they can compare the writing of the homework and the death threat. If the handwriting on the note and the homework match, the child can no longer be in your classroom. Call you teachers' union at any point if you need more support.

Fight for your rights if you are suspended from your job. Situation: an administrator comes into your classroom and tells you to report to the head secretary's office after school because the district is putting you on indefinite leave. They will not tell you why.

You finish teaching your classes for the day and are shaken up. You walk to the head secretary's office. They tell you to report to the human resources department at the district office immediately. Your secretary is vague and says the issue has something to do with your fingerprints. When you ask them what you can do about it, they give you a phone number to the state department of education.

As you drive there, you are puzzled. You renewed your license at the earliest possible moment nine months before the expiration date. A new state policy has just gone into effect: new fingerprints are now required every time you renew your license. Prior to this, fingerprints were only required when you first got a job in the state.

You redid your fingerprints as part of the new process. The person doing them told you most of your fingerprints had indistinct ridges. Because of many years as a hairdresser prior to teaching, working with chemicals, they have worn off. You even called the department of education a few weeks later because of what the person doing your fingerprints told you; when you received a renewal of your license in hard copy, the department said the fingerprints were fine.

You walk into the human resources department. The supervisor tells you not to step foot on your school campus until this is settled. You are placed on leave without pay and your case is under investigation. You ask how long you will be out. You are told it could be weeks or months even. The gravity of the situation has hit you and you start sobbing. The supervisor walks you to the door and tells you to leave.

You go home and cry for hours. You are humiliated and charged without due process. You are angry because your students will not have their regular teacher. You call your teachers' union. They say they cannot help you because it is out of their jurisdiction. They tell you to call them after it is over and tell them how it went. What do you do now?

You get on the phone and call the state department of education. You only get an answering machine. You try several more times with the same result, and then you get up your nerve. You leave a message about your situation and end with: "I am a veteran law-abiding teacher with top evaluations. I will hire a lawyer to defend me if you do not resolve this immediately." That gets their attention. You receive a phone call.

There has been a series of errors: The state had failed to notify the district you were out of compliance due to indistinct fingerprints and needed to redo your fingerprints by a certain due date. The district failed to notify you because they never received the e-mail. The school failed to notify you because they never received the e-mail from the district.

The next day, your administrator calls you, says the situation has been resolved, and tells you to return to school immediately. It is 10 a.m. and you are still in your pajamas after being up all night. You tell them you need two hours to get ready, and you take them. You are angry that you had to do all the work to exonerate yourself and they demand you return immediately after everything you have been through. You slowly get dressed and take yourself out to a clothing store to buy something nice for you.

You return to school and tell your students what happened and why their teacher has been absent. You feel they deserve an explanation. Some parents e-mail you to express their support. One student will send you a note at the end of the year saying they think you are the bravest teacher they have ever known.

You never call the union to tell them how it went. You drop your membership in the teachers' union in anger because they said they could not help you when you were suspended from your job.

When you call your local union about dropping your membership, they say there is only a small window once a year within thirty days when you can drop your membership. You must wait until then and send a signed letter stating you are dropping your union membership. You can sign up for union membership at any time, but you can only drop once a year. You decide to rejoin several years later, reminding yourself the union works hard for teacher contracts and does not represent just you but all teachers in the District.

Six years later, you must renew your license due to state teacher licensure rules. This requires a new set of fingerprints. You go to a different place and are also told your finger ridges are worn down but still readable. The operator says her mom, a nurse who worked with her hands, has the same issue. She tells you technology has improved, and she thinks the fingerprints will be accepted. You immediately call the state education department and tell them they must call you once they receive your fingerprints because you are not going through what you went through six years ago. Your fingerprints are accepted this time.

Get support from the administration when you need it. A teacher once had a difficult student who would not cooperate and came tardy to class daily, squeaking their boots across the floor for their grand entrance. The student repeatedly interrupted their class.

When the teacher went to an administrator for help, they were told it was their fault because they did not know how to control their class. They said to the administrator, "Do not speak to me like this. You know I am a strict teacher with excellent classroom management. I have never before asked you for help." The administrator then agreed to write up a behavior contract for the student that the administrator had to supervise.

Fight for your rights when you are bullied. Situation: an itinerant art teacher is teaching a sixth-grade art class. The students swear at them and throw objects at their feet. The teacher goes to an administrator and they refuse to discuss it with the teacher, saying the teacher is not a regular teacher at the school so they do not have to handle this.

In desperation, the teacher videotapes the students swearing at them and objects being thrown at their feet. Then they ask for a meeting with the administrator. They bring the tape recorder, and the administrator will not listen to it. They call their district art supervisor on the phone and tell them they are quitting this part of their job and the supervisor can deduct the pay from their paycheck.

The supervisor is worried because it is mid-year, and they have no new hire available to take this part of the job if the teacher quits. They send in a veteran art teacher from the district, and they team teach the rest of the year. The students' behavior does improve.

The art teacher has their own children at home zoned for the school where the situation with the administrator occurred. They request a variance. They do not want their children going to a school where the teachers are not respected by the administration.

Know your teacher contract. Situation: a parent calls a school counselor at your school and requests their child have study hall every day at lunch because they do not have time at home to study and complete homework due to extracurricular activities. The school counselor e-mails their five teachers and requests each of them take the child one day a week in their classroom at lunch for study hall. The other four teachers agree.

You e-mail the counselor and say this is out of compliance with your contract: teachers daily have thirty minutes duty-free lunch. The counselor writes you back and says they do not think that is correct. You immediately e-mail the teacher union representative in your building about the situation. The representative corrects the guidance counselor, and they withdraw their request.

Know your teacher rights. Assembly Bill 521 (AB521), also known as the Student Discipline Bill, was signed into Nevada state law by then governor Kenny Guinn in June of 1999. It was sponsored by the NSEA (Nevada State Education Association).

This law gives teachers the authority to remove disruptive students from their classrooms. This is a legally authorized shift in authority from administrators to teachers in making some decisions about students. This came about after a poll was taken in February of 1998 where 70 percent of NSEA members said being able to remove disruptive students from their classrooms was a high priority.

Some NSEA members testified in front of the legislature that when they sent disruptive students to the office, often they were returned with nothing done to address the students' behavior. Ken Lange, then executive director of NSEA wrote, "Education Reform takes place in the classroom. If teachers cannot teach because of disruption in their classroom, then students aren't learning."

The law states the principal of every school must establish a plan for progressive discipline with the input and participation of teachers and parents. The law applies to special education students if the plan to remove the student complies with all federal laws and regulations and district policies relating to children with disabilities. The plan must provide for the temporary removal of a pupil from the classroom to an alternate placement.

Here are the steps:

1. A teacher follows the progressive discipline plan with a student who constantly disrupts the class. Nothing works. The teacher decides to invoke AB521.
2. The teacher removes the student from the class and notifies the principal this is an AB521 referral.
3. The principal must explain to the student why they were removed from the class and give the student an opportunity to respond.
4. The principal must notify the parents about the student's removal within twenty-four hours.
5. The student is assigned to a temporary alternate location where they are separated from other students, monitored while they study alone by an appropriate district person, and not allowed to engage in any extracurricular activities.
6. A conference must be held within three school days with the student, parents or guardians, teacher, and principal. If the parent refuses to respond to the notification of the conference or refuses to attend the conference, they will have waived their right to a conference, and the principal will make a recommendation about the placement of the student.

7. After the conference, the principal will recommend whether to return the student to the classroom or to continue the temporary placement.
8. If they recommend the student return to the classroom and the teacher disagrees, the principal will call a meeting of the Placement Review Committee, a committee composed of the principal and two teachers selected by most of the teachers who are at the school, and inform the parents the committee will meet to discuss the student's placement.
9. The committee reviews the circumstances of the pupil's removal and decides on the best placement. The committee has five options: send the student back to the teacher's class, assign the student to another appropriate class, assign the student to an alternative program of education if available, recommend suspension or expulsion, or take any other appropriate disciplinary action against the student that the committee deems necessary.

This law let students and parents know teachers oversaw their classes. This law is no longer used. Newer teachers are not familiar with it after twenty years, and administrators do not use it, even though it is still on the books. Go to https://www.leg.state.nv.us for more information (Assembly Bill 521 1998).

A curious twist: one issue of this law was that it only applied to the classroom. S.B.386(R1) was introduced to the Nevada legislature in 2017, as an extension of AB521, to apply to all the school facilities, for example, the school bus, the school cafeteria, and the hallways. Each of these areas needed the progressive discipline plan. It was approved by Governor Sandoval on June 3, 2017.

In recent years, the protocol at some schools is: The teacher turns in their syllabus at the beginning of the year with their progressive discipline plan. If there is a chronic behavioral issue during the year, the teacher needs to document how they followed through with their progressive discipline plan each step of the way, and then if things are not improving, they call the principal on their classroom phone. The principal comes down and meets the teacher and student outside of the classroom to discuss the situation.

Some concerns with this procedure are: First, the rest of the class is left unattended while this discussion goes on and valuable learning time is lost. Second, this could easily turn into a he said/she said situation where the student is on the same level as the teacher.

The parties should be spoken with separately for each version of the story, not during class time, and then the administrator should set up a meeting including the parents. Of course, this takes more time, but the goal here is not efficiency for the administrator. The teacher has put up with unacceptable behavior for quite a while most likely due to the progressive discipline plan. Quite a change from the AB521 where the teacher oversaw the classroom.

Join an empowering teachers' group in your state, if you have one. Empower Nevada Teachers (ENT) was started by teachers in the Washoe County School District. It is not affiliated with any union or political party. Its only agenda is to support teachers in the community and across the state of Nevada.

If you do not have an empowering teachers' group in your state, start one yourself with other teachers in your area. Here are some of the goals of ENT: (1) smaller class sizes; (2) increase per pupil spending; (3) wear red on Wednesdays; (4) make education seen (support, educate, empower); (5) give teachers a living wage; (6) develop community partnerships; and (7) grassroots movements (Empower Nevada Teachers 2019).

Consider joining your local teachers, union, which bargains on your behalf for better wages, benefits, and working conditions in your district. According to an online article by FindLaw, entitled "Teachers' Unions and Collective Bargaining: Overview" (2016), "Teachers, like other public employees, do not have the constitutional right to collectively bargain (that is for the states to decide). However, the First Amendment does provide that people have the right to 'peaceably assemble,' which includes the right to join a union (if not as a vehicle for collective bargaining). Also, teachers do not have the constitutional right to go on strike, although that right may be granted through other federal or state laws" (FindLaw 2016).

In an online article written on February 28, 2019, entitled "Rebuilding Public Education Is Essential to Saving America," author John Grossenbacher, the past director of the US Department of Energy's Idaho National Laboratory, mentions America's public education system depends on American values and it is our most important infrastructure. He says it is in serious need of repair: "Public education in America replaced a traditional system of educating children that relied entirely on family, church, community, and apprenticeship. It has always been highly decentralized, with local governments and institutions responsible for school funding and control. The federal government did not get involved in public education . . . until the civil rights movement sparked concerns about educational equity. Simultaneously, technological competition with The Soviet Union caused us to worry they were getting ahead of us in science and mathematics."

Grossenbacher believes,

> As the world became more connected and economically competitive, educational excellence and educational equity were rallying points for educational reform. School boards, local governments, philanthropists, and the federal government all responded with reform initiatives.
>
> Today, teachers and their unions are under attack, accused of being barriers to improvement and accountability. Their defenders counter that poor student performance is rooted in poverty, family, and societal breakdown and that the teachers and their unions are scapegoats. Charter schools, vouchers, and parental choice are necessary, advocates say, to compel our reform-resistant school system to change. Opponents believe these initiatives promote privatization and private-sector profits while undermining universally available quality public education.

Grossenbacher writes,

> The federal government is not capable of leading a public education reformation. Its attempts at standards-based reforms, No Child Left Behind (Bush) and Race to the Top (Obama), are case studies in federal limitations. Our schools must be reformed from the bottom up and within, driven by parents and teachers. . . . Each state's public universities should be assigned the mission of joining the effort. By formally partnering with their school boards, providing educational expertise, collecting data, and offering analysis, they can add more local capability to reform and improvement efforts.
>
> Our public universities, school boards, teachers, and parents are our best chance at reforming and reinventing America's public education system. . . . Growing class divisions and isolation, hyper individualism and aversion to sacrificing in the short term to invest for the future are national behaviors that stand in our way.

John Adams once said, "No expense for this purpose would be thought extravagant," regarding public education.

Grossenbacher concludes, "The idea is America depends on educated citizens. It depends on their holding values of fairness, generosity, and hopefulness" (Grossenbacher 2019).

The Federal contribution to K–12 education is about 8 percent, which includes funds from the Department of Education and other federal agencies like the Department of Health and Human Services Head Start Program and the Department of Agriculture's School Lunch Program.

In her book, *The Death and Life of the Great American School System: How Testing and Choice Are Undermining Education*, Diane Ravitch, former US assistant secretary of education, says the teachers' unions are not the problem. She cites Finland, the nation with the highest test scores in the world, as 100 percent union. She thinks the very conservative right-wing governors want to break the unions because "the unions provide support to the Democratic Party. But the unions aren't the problem in education" (Ravitch 2011).

If you sign up for a union membership, you are automatically a member of the state-level union. Every state has at least one state-level affiliate—either the American Federation of Teachers (AFT) or the National Educators Association (NEA). The largest union in the United States is the NEA. Formed in 1857, it functions more as a professional organization and tends to be suburban. The second largest union in the United States is the AFT. Formed in 1916, it functions more like a labor union and tends to be urban. Both organizations tend to support Democratic ideologies.

There will be a monthly fee withdrawn from your paycheck for union dues if you are a union member.

Teacher union membership is not mandatory anymore due to two Supreme Court rulings. In 1977, *Abood v. Detroit Board of Education* ruled unions could only collect fees necessary for salary negotiations, even if a teacher did not join the union. In 2018, *Abood v. Detroit* was overturned; the court declared the original ruling was "poorly reasoned and lacked workability."

Janus v. AFSCME, a case involving an Illinois social worker, stated all public employees (not just teachers) must choose to support the union before any money is taken from them. The reason is the First Amendment right to free speech is violated when public employees are forced to give money to organizations whose views they might not support.

The ruling came after union-supported teacher walkouts in six states that resulted in teachers getting raises and more education funds from conservative lawmakers. According to *The New York Times* online article on June 27, 2018, entitled, "What the Supreme Court's *Janus* Decision Means for Teachers Unions," *Janus* was funded by President Trump and his conservative allies. They did not want public employees having a professional voice and decision-making power as represented by their unions.

Randi Weingarten, president of the AFT, stated regarding Trump and his allies and their effect on teachers: "These folks that have huge power over their lives have tried to cut school budgets, tried to hurt their health care, cut retirement benefits, privatize hospitals and schools, are now having the chutzpah to say give up your Union to get a quick raise. People are getting it big time and are basically trying to stick with the union."

Randi Weingarten remains optimistic: of 800,000 AFT members in eighteen states affected by the *Janus* decision, AFT had secured more than 500,000 recommitments to retain membership since January 2019. Lily Eskelsen García, president of the NEA at that time, said the *Janus* decision could mean a loss of up to 200,000 members: $28 million less in the organization's $366 million budget.

The NEA is preparing to reach out to younger teachers who do not have deep loyalties to organized labor. This *Janus* ruling could weaken all teacher unions across the United States if memberships go down. In 2015–2016, 70 percent of US teachers belonged to a union, down from 79 percent in 1999–2000 (Goldstein and Green 2018; Kelly 2020).

According to the FindLaw article mentioned earlier, teachers' unions also handle grievances that deal with contract violations, provide training, lobby federal and state lawmakers, and work to improve education quality for all students (such as reducing class size and improving curriculum). Unions may also collectively bargain on behalf of teachers for academic freedom, curriculum, wages, benefits, hours, workload, responsibilities, tenure, promotion, evaluation procedures, retirement and pension benefits, and vacation and sick leave (FindLaw 2016).

According to an online article by ThoughtCo. on January 6, 2019, entitled "Pros and Cons of Joining a Teachers Union" (Meador 2019), the advantages to joining include legal protection and advice; support, guidance, and advice in the form of classes or a phone hotline; a voice in hot educational trends, debates, and topics you feel strongly about; and collective bargaining on behalf of teachers for contract and labor negotiations.

Also, teachers' unions can provide discount programs at specified stores, information on life insurance benefits and credit card opportunities, mortgage assistance, and legal assistance not related to your career, such as drawing up wills or living trusts.

Reasons for not joining the teachers' union could include: you do not agree with the union politics, union fees are expensive especially for first-year teachers who have the lowest salary, and you do not believe you need it.

Be careful thinking you do not need it. A newer teacher may lack the confidence to stand their ground. Union representation may be necessary to save their job if they are challenged. Also, supporting the union is a support not just for you but for all teachers (Meador 2019).

In an online article on TeacherFreedom.org entitled "Your Education Association Rights" (2020), they remind teachers your employer cannot discriminate against you based on your union membership status. The terms of the negotiated agreement apply to you regardless of your union membership status, and if you opt out of the teachers' union, you will not lose your teaching contract, seniority, or other benefits.

Your job seniority and tenure are protected by your contract and state and federal law. Additional protection is also available through nonunion education associates. Some alternative national and state nonunion associates are the Association of American Educators, Christian Educators Association International, Associated Professional Educators of Louisiana, and Arkansas State Teachers Association. For more information, check the TeacherFreedom.org website and article mentioned above.

Note that TeacherFreedom.org is an antiunion organization that says they offer benefits in proportion with union membership. However, they are not the bargaining unit of the teachers' contract and are not physically present in many areas to provide representation when it is needed. Also, do your homework and make sure you understand what political or social agendas each of these organizations supports before considering membership ("Your Education Association Rights" 2020).

Public-school teachers are on probation for a certain number of years depending on the state when they are first hired. According to the online article "Teacher Rights," a probationary teacher can be dismissed if it does not involve discrimination (based on race, color, religion, sex, or national origin of the teacher) or violate terms of the teacher's contract. The school district probably does not need to provide notice, summary of charges, or a hearing to the teacher (Glink 2018).

In Nevada, teachers are on probation for their first three years; they have more frequent and intense evaluations, have no right to continued employment after any school year, and have limited procedural rights if they are suspended or dismissed during a school year.

Once a teacher is off probation, they are postprobationary status. There is no tenure. Postprobationary teachers have due process rights if they are to be dismissed, demoted, or refused a contract for the next school year. Every teacher in Nevada signs one-year contracts with the local district (Washoe Education Association 2020; "There's a Reason Tenure Cannot Be Taken from a Nevada Public School Teacher, and It's Simple" 2015).

According to the above article on teacher rights (Glink 2018), a school must show cause to dismiss a teacher who is not on probation. Some causes for dismissal include immoral conduct, incompetence, neglect of duty, substantial noncompliance with school laws, conviction of a crime, insubordination, and fraud or misrepresentation.

The due process clause of the Fourteenth Amendment says that no state may "deprive any person of life, liberty, or property, without due process of law." Due process means a postprobationary teacher must be given oral or written notice of the dismissal and the charges against them with an explanation of the evidence obtained by the employer and an opportunity for a fair and meaningful hearing.

Teachers have limited academic freedoms in the classroom to teach on the content or subjects for discussion. These freedoms are based on the freedom of expression under the First Amendment. However, the content taught must be relevant to and consistent with the teacher's responsibilities. A teacher cannot promote a personal or political agenda in the classroom. Also factored into the teacher's academic freedom are the age, experience, and grade level of the students.

Teachers have the right to freedom of association due to the First Amendment, which grants citizens the right to peaceful assembly. Teachers can join professional organizations like teachers' unions or run for public office. However, these activities must be completely independent from their responsibilities at school.

Teachers have the right to freedom of religion due to the First Amendment. However, public schools are restricted from teaching religion through the Establishment Clause of the First Amendment. For example, a teacher is free to be a practicing Christian, but they cannot preach Christianity in the classroom.

Teachers have limited rights to personal privacy. However, courts will support disciplinary action by a school district when the teacher's private life affects the integrity of the school district or the effectiveness of a teacher to teach (Glink 2018).

Think before you post on social media. Even if you use privacy settings and do not befriend students or their parents, a photo or comment could be copied or captured via a screenshot and made public. Check if your district has rules or policies regarding social media, and make sure you comply with them.

The Age Discrimination in Employment Act of 1967 provides protection for teachers over the age of forty against age discrimination. Age may not be the only reason a school terminates the employment of a teacher. If a teacher charges a school district with age discrimination, the school district must prove some factor other than age caused their decision.

The Pregnancy Discrimination Act of 1978 protects pregnant teachers. Under this act, a school district cannot dismiss, demote, nor deny a job or promotion to a pregnant teacher (Glink 2018).

12

PATIENT: GROWING FROM EXPERIENCES

Be patient with yourself. Anything you are passionate about takes work, and you will have your good and your bad days. When you first begin teaching, you may doubt yourself after a bad day and think you should give up. However, much of teaching is on-the-job training, and you will get savvier with experience.

It could take you three to five years before you feel confident about being a teacher. Do not give up. No one is born a natural teacher. Some people are more comfortable, but everyone must work at it. There are no shortcuts. You practice and practice. You learn from mistakes and you grow.

Be realistic: you are not a superhero. You cannot save every child from situations that are beyond your control, such as family dynamics. You want to help your students find their voice and stand up for themselves. Teachers need to not wear themselves out getting heavily involved in matters they have no business pursuing. This is not professional.

If a student does share information with you that they are endangered, you have a professional responsibility to report it in time with your district rules. Usually that is within twenty-four hours. Report issues to child protective services, school counselors, and the principal. If you feel overwhelmed, get professional help for yourself.

One of the worst situations to ever deal with is when one of your current students dies. If it happens after school, probably an administrator will call you at home to break the news. The next day, a guidance counselor will most likely come into your classroom to observe the students.

If you have no idea how to proceed with your classes, ask the guidance counselor to step outside with you and seek their help. Ask them for guidance on what to say and do for the student's family. Maybe the guidance counselor could speak directly to your class or the two of you could present something together. This is not a normal day, and care must be taken so you do not appear insensitive to the situation when you feel awkward, upset, and unsure what to do.

You could send a card to the family from just you or from you and the student's classmates, perhaps sharing favorite memories of their child so they know their child will live on in the hearts of others. You could leave the child's desk empty for a few weeks in honor of them to show they matter and are not replaceable. Eventually you could change everyone's seats to give you all a fresh start and not have an empty desk. Some students may drop your class because it reminds them daily of their grief. Try not to take it personally. It is your job now to patiently rebuild your community classroom.

You may have medical emergencies in your classroom. A student could suddenly go into convulsions during your class. You may witness them hit their head on the floor and then their eyes roll up into their head. You are not a doctor and should not attempt to handle this on your own.

Always keep an emergency number and what information to say in an emergency taped next to your classroom phone. Even a memorized number can go out of your head in a serious situation. Your hands may be shaking as you pick up the phone, but force yourself to speak calmly and slowly to not frighten your students.

The person responding will tell you what to do before they arrive. Move your students away from the child. An emergency team made up of trained teachers and administrators in your building will be in your classroom within minutes. They will take over once they arrive. If possible, have a next-door colleague take your entire class inside their room, so they are not standing out in the hall and getting in the way of emergency personnel and equipment. There is no roadmap in teaching: you never arrive and know it all. You do the best you can each day.

Teaching takes a lot of patience. Assess if this is truly the career for you before you become committed. Observe teachers in their classrooms and interview them about their careers before deciding to major in education. Even ask if you can assist them with an activity to get a feel for the job. Real-life teaching is not as it is portrayed on television.

Nowadays college students are doing practicums in their sophomore years or earlier. In previous decades, education majors did not enter classrooms until their senior year of college when they student taught.

Part III

Creating Success after Retiring from Teaching

13

BE PRESENT TO THE END OF YOUR CAREER AND RETIRE ON YOUR TERMS

This is your last year! There are no more dress rehearsals. Every lesson is the last time you will ever teach it. Savor every minute of it. Arrive early to school every day and walk up the front steps in gratitude for being at your school and being appreciated by the staff and students. In the early morning silence, go through the lessons you will teach for the day and the necessary setup.

It is your chance to become even more joyful in teaching and more determined that every student has the right to learn. Sign up for anything extracurricular that has meaning for you. Your last year is your legacy or gift to the future of your current students. Serve on the school scholarship committee and call out students' names at the high school graduation. You are graduating and so are your students.

Retire on your terms. If the administration asks you to take on a student teacher your last year and you do not want someone else teaching because you want the final year of students all to yourself, tell the administration. If, on the other hand, you want a student teacher, make sure you tell them.

Be aware in the last semester that as you transition, so does the environment around you. Staff may be thinking ahead. Do not be surprised if they start discussing who will get your room, what furniture they would like, and so on. In your head, you get it, but in your heart, it hurts. Maybe you should be thanking them in your head because they are helping you cut the umbilical cord. Focus on the future.

However, if it does start to affect how you view your job, set a date, maybe a month before you retire, and e-mail your staff when they can come down to your room and go through your furniture. That way you oversee your exit and not your colleagues. Another thought: colleagues can claim dibs on your furniture a month before you retire, but maybe ask them not to take the items until after the last day of school so you and your students are not upset about an empty room.

Be present until the end. Do not let up on your students. Have the same expectations. As to when to tell them you are retiring, that is up to you. Some teachers tell their students at the beginning of their last year. Some teachers tell the parents at Open House of their last year. In any case, when you do decide to tell everyone, tell them you are excited for an amazing last year and recite the projects and activities you will be doing. In other words, full steam ahead.

There are also teachers who prefer not to tell their students or parents at all because they are concerned they will be written off as a lame duck teacher and not respected. Colleagues need to honor the retiring teacher's wishes: if they want to keep their retirement a secret, colleagues should not be telling their students that said teacher is retiring.

Once you retire, you will be cut out of your district e-mail. It might seem like you never existed. To return to school to volunteer post-retirement, you will need to get a badge and sign in just like all visitors. You want that. That is for the safety of your school.

When you retire, you are present to yourself more than you ever were before. When you had a job, you compartmentalized your feelings, and could only deal with them when you were not at your job. Now you are your feelings' captive audience if you do not set boundaries. You will probably go through lots of feelings when you retire. Be aware of them and accept them, but do not bury them in fear. Understand you do not have to dwell on the negative ones every minute. If it gets to be too much and you are suppressing your feelings with alcohol, food, TV, and so on, see a professional mental health specialist.

Some of the possible feelings may be: first, you may feel the joy of freedom. When that wears off, you may have anxiety and depression because teachers are used to fast-paced lives, quick decisions, and always being on stage. You may feel like a hamster on a wheel and feel you must keep busy.

Some teachers in the first three months of their retirement might clean out all their closets and repaint every room in their house. They simply cannot sit still. Others may be able to let go of the school schedule, not thinking what class they would be teaching at which time, but have trouble getting off the stage: they are so used to very busy being their normal and they have so many hobbies, they do not give themselves a day off until they realize they are burning themselves out. Give yourself permission to take a day off and do nothing if that is what you need. Some retired people even schedule days off in their calendars. Not a bad idea.

Some retired teachers still operate in teacher decision mode where everything must be decided right now. Learn to prioritize and accept it is okay to leave not-as-important decisions for tomorrow or the next day. You always had long to-do lists as a teacher, but you do not have to continue that practice into retirement.

Same idea: it is fine to have a list, but it is okay if everything is not completed on it today because it gives you something to do tomorrow. Another thing that can really help you is to find something that grounds and soothes you—something you can get lost in and something you enjoy—for example: cooking, walking outside in nature, reading, yoga, and participating in sports and music.

14

PREPARE FINANCIALLY AND EMOTIONALLY FOR RETIREMENT

Do not wait until you retire to figure out how you will fill your time. Start moving in that direction three to five years before you retire. Read retirement books such as *How to Retire Happy, Wild, and Free* by Ernie J. Zelinski. One of the best things mentioned in the book is creating your Ultimate Life Adventure List, aka Get-A-Life Tree. The directions are to make a list of twenty-five to fifty things to do that would excite you and try to get at least five items in each category.

Do not worry about how to attain or achieve them—no reasoning or doubting can affect your list. Do not worry how many of them you will accomplish. Suggested categories are: adventure and special experiences, ways to make a difference, special people to meet, exotic travel destinations, skills to learn, and special things to buy (Zelinski 2009).

At first, you may be stumped and think of yourself as a boring person, but as you get into it—and it does take some time—you will really have fun with it! Post it on your refrigerator, and on days where you doubt yourself, reread your answers and realize you have a lot to look forward to in retirement.

Perhaps you will travel to countries you always planned to visit but never got around to when you were working full time. You can make a difference by writing a book or volunteering in your community. The new skills you will pick up from these experiences can be exciting and invigorating. You may meet special people like established authors and community leaders who inspire you. You might buy yourself a special gift like a milk frother because you enjoy frothy milk with your coffee first thing every morning as you read the newspaper.

In an online article written by journalist Jonathan Burton in 2019 entitled "You're Probably Not Ready to Retire—Psychologically," he wrote that your emotional plan for retirement is just as important as your financial plan. He said many preretirees do not fully understand how their lives will change when they retire. Retirement is a leap of faith from a familiar life of routine to a new unknown life that will take six to eight years of transition before it is your new normal.

According to Ken Dychtwald, a gerontologist and the coauthor of the best-seller *Age Wave*, there are five stages of retirement: imagination, anticipation, liberation, reorientation, and reconciliation. Stage 1, imagination, is fifteen to five years before retirement. It is a time of fantasies, hopes, and wishes. It gives you something to look forward to, especially on tough workdays.

Or perhaps you never think about retirement until five years before you retire. It scares you to think about it. You do not have fantasies and big dreams ahead. You loved your career so much; you feel sad and an empty feeling in the pit of your stomach when you think about retirement. You think about all the students you will never get to meet or teach.

Stage 2, anticipation, is five years prior to retirement. It is reality. You look around and you see friends and colleagues retiring. The finish line is in sight for you. Some people are tired of working at this point. It is time to seek advice on how to handle emotionally retiring. Financially, there is plenty of advice on how to retire, but emotionally, not so much. Retirement coach Mitch Anthony believes people decide when to retire based on finances rather than their mental health. But being emotionally grounded going into retirement will likely lead to better financial decisions in retirement (Burton 2019).

Perhaps you get to the anticipation stage when your spouse retires a year before you. You are seeing retirement in real time, and you are starting to like it. It is not the end of the world. Retired friends start calling you and suggest you join their bowling league after retirement. You think, what a great way to make new friends and have something to work at. You are not a great bowler, but so what? How liberating to try something, and if you do not like it, you could always quit.

Stage 3, liberation, is the first year of retirement. Nancy Schlossberg, author of *Too Young to Be Old: Love, Learn, Work, and Play as You Age*, has identified several types of retirees: adventurers who shake things up, searchers looking to fit in, easy gliders who live one day at a time, involved spectators who are still connected to their careers, and retreaters: those who pause to regroup and those who never leave their rocking chair. You may be a combination of these types in your first year. This is the honeymoon phase when everything is new (Burton 2019).

Perhaps the first year you are an adventurer: you say yes to anything that interests you, even if you have never done it before. So what if you stay up late or must get up early? No problem because you do not have to be in top form to go to work the next day. You could also be an involved spectator by choice: you love going to your former high school to guest speak, coach, or attend social functions with your former colleagues. You are not hanging on because you are afraid to disconnect—you really loved your former job and love helping and being around friends.

Stage 4, reorientation, is two to fifteen years after retirement. The honeymoon is over. You are settling into your new normal. You start paying attention to your legacy. Your legacy is not the material wealth you will leave in a will; it is how you will be remembered. It is a chance to distribute the wealth of knowledge, depth, and wisdom you have acquired just by being alive. You realize you have something to offer the world. You do not just become elderly; you become an elder—wise and experienced. You can mentor people career-wise or life-wise (Burton 2019).

Perhaps you are writing a book because you loved teaching. Writing the book, you are still teaching. It is a different form. You are not in the classroom anymore, but you are sharing your love, knowledge, and experience as a veteran teacher. You must write this book. That is how much teaching meant and still means to you.

The fifth and final stage, reconciliation, is more than fifteen years after retirement. Reconciliation means to restore harmony after conflict. After years of transformation in these retirement stages, you accept who you are and where you are because you have a new identity outside of your job that brings you meaning and purpose (Burton 2019).

Do not wait until you retire to figure out your finances. The time to start saving for retirement is when you get your first job! Speak with your district or a financial planner about depositing money every month into a retirement account. It may not be much at first, but it all adds up. Increase your contribution as your salary goes up.

Visit with your district retirement system specialists five years before you retire. They figure out based on your current salary at that time how much you will receive in retirement. When you retire, your goal is to live within your means. You may decide to work or not to work.

Write down your usual monthly expenditures on one side of a piece of paper and then decide if there are any expenses you could live without. For example, you could sell your trailer—and get out of monthly payments—because you realize you are not using it anymore after your children moved out. You could switch to a gym that charges less per month. As your children get full-time jobs, they can take over their own car insurance, health insurance, and phone bills.

You must be honest—if there is something that is important to you, then do not cut it out, because retirement is about having and doing things that are meaningful for you. For example, if you try to cut the golf channel but are miserable, reinstate it. You might cut out your local newspaper subscription because it is too expensive. You then realize it is important to you and find the perfect compromise: purchase the online edition, which is cheaper and does not waste paper.

At the beginning of the month after paying your required bills, put a predetermined amount of whatever is left over into savings and the rest is fun money. That way you do not feel guilty about spending money.

If possible, find a fellow colleague retiring the same year you are. Go through this change together instead of alone. Remind each other of deadlines like submitting resignation letters. Blow off steam together when the going gets tough and remind each other this will not matter next year. Gloat privately (not in front of other teachers) on days you are excited about your new and upcoming life. Plan a retirement celebration together or separately.

15

PART OF A NEW TEAM AND NEW INTERESTS

When you retire, you have more time to help your family, if that is something you want to do. The satisfaction of helping an elderly parent with chores or playing and taking care of a grandchild can be very enriching for you. You are making a difference in a loved one's life. Again, make sure you establish boundaries, so you have time for yourself and this does not become a full-time job.

When you retire, your team, colleagues from school, will most likely not stay in touch with you. They are busy in their job world, and you are no longer a part of it. You need to move on. In an April 23, 2019, online article from the National Institute on Aging, entitled "Social Isolation, Loneliness in Older People Pose Health Risks," researchers studied the difference between social isolation and loneliness and how to help people affected by these conditions.

According to the late Dr. John Cacioppo, former director of the Center for Cognitive and Social Neuroscience at the University of Chicago, social isolation is, "the objective physical separation from other people (living alone), while loneliness is the subjective distressed feeling of being alone or separated. It is possible to feel lonely while among other people, and you can be alone yet not feeling lonely."

Social isolation and loneliness have been linked to higher risks for high blood pressure, heart disease, obesity, anxiety, depression, cognitive decline, Alzheimer's disease, and even death. People who are suddenly alone due to the death of a spouse or partner, separation from friends or family, retirement, loss of mobility, or lack of transportation are especially at risk. Losing a sense of connection and community changes a person's perspective of the world.

Chronic loneliness makes a person feel threatened and mistrustful of others. Their world shrinks because they spend most of their time in their home managing their household and their health. They are afraid to show they need help because they fear they will be forced to move from their homes, which is all they have.

On the other hand, people who engage in meaningful, productive activities with others tend to live longer, have a boosted mood, and have a sense of purpose. These activities maintain well-being, develop a greater sense of community, and may also improve cognitive function (National Institute on Aging 2019).

If you are unsure where to begin, call an organization you are passionate about: for example, the SPCA, and find out in which areas they need volunteers. There may be an organization in your city for retired teachers who meet several times a year to socialize and fund scholarships for children of current teachers in the district.

Many cities have a newcomers club that is not just for new people to the area. It is also for people who are beginning new parts of their lives. Remember, one of the benefits of being retired is you get to try new things, and if they do not appeal to you, it is okay to walk away and try something else. Start with small changes to your daily retired routine and add on as your interests grow. You will learn new facets of yourself.

16

POSITIVE: RETIREMENT IS AN ATTITUDE AND NOT AN EVENT

There is life after a teaching career if you had a life during your teaching career. Do not assume when you retire that you will run off into happily ever after. Retirement is an attitude and not an event. If you were a grumpy teacher with nothing besides your job, expect to be a grumpy retiree with nothing to do. Take up hobbies long before you retire. Challenge yourself further by joining, for example, a bowling team, a local choir, or a book club when you retire. If you were an energetic and positive teacher, you can remain that same person today.

17

PROACTIVE LEADER: CREATE WHAT YOU WANT TO HAPPEN IN RETIREMENT

Create what you want to happen in retirement. You are the author of your life script now. Do not be a reactor waiting for life to happen. When you worked, you had a routine: alarm goes off, shower, get dressed, eat breakfast, make a lunch, and head out the door. As you transition to retirement, a schedule might bring you comfort because routine is familiar to you.

Try different activities for your routine. For example, start the morning with frothy milk and the newspaper. Then practice your trumpet for an hour or so. Go to the gym and exercise five to seven days a week. Socialize with friends in your spinning classes at the gym, but also meet friends several times a month for lunch. Cook every other night (make enough food for two days in a row) for your spouse and sometimes for relatives and friends. Remember to break out of the routine every now and then just to go to the beach for the day or go out on a date night.

Make sure to still plan vacations. Even though you are retired, you still need a vacation from your retirement. Go places outside of your community and come back refreshed.

18

PATIENT IN YOUR TRANSITION TO RETIREMENT

Some people struggle and lose their way in retirement. They worry about not having a purpose. Forget about purpose and find what interests you. If you do not know, that is even better. Try things and do not worry about being the best. Your interests will become your purpose down the road. Spend time in nature. Take time to recover from a hectic career. Give yourself permission to slow down.

A yoga teacher once said, "Live in your bubble and never compare yourself to someone else." Another retired friend may have gobs of fun pictures on Facebook and look like they have retirement all figured out, but that does not mean they do not have days of doubt, just like you.

CONCLUSION

Leading Changes from the Classroom

The idea of teacher leadership is not new: teachers have served as team leaders, department chairs, union representatives, curriculum developers, and mentors. These roles were at the discretion of school administrators. Teachers were representatives of the administration but not leaders enacting change. Teachers had little control in decision-making yet were responsible for the product (student learning). In a 2014 Gallup Poll, of twelve surveyed professions, teachers were least likely to agree with the statement "My opinion seems to matter at work." Leadership meant leaving teaching and going into administration.

In the 1970s in New York City, a movement began for educators to remain in the classroom but be part of the decision-making process and not just give input. This movement is called teacher-led or teacher-powered schools. This movement could apply to an entire school, a department, or a program within the school. This is a deliberate change in mindset. It cannot be a random one-day activity here and there. It must be intentionally embedded and worded into the school's vision.

It is defined as autonomy for teachers to design and run schools with the aim of increased student learning and achievement individually or collectively. This could include the areas of curriculum, budget, selecting personnel, scheduling, teacher evaluations, instructional planning and resources, work hours and tenure policy, school discipline, professional development, and school furniture.

It could also include teachers deciding who enters the profession and based on what criterion. Greater autonomy is also accepting accountability for school success (Teacher-Powered Schools 2020; Alvarez 2015; Manno 2019; Haigler 2018).

One step further could be collaboration of teachers, administrators, and unions. Saul Rubinstein, a professor in the School of Management and Labor Relations at Rutgers University and the director of its Program on Collaborative School Reform, has focused his research in the past on labor-management efforts to transform industries. Together with John McCarthy, assistant professor at Cornell University, he focused in 2011 on reforming public schools through sustained union-management collaboration. They have published two reports and proven how this collaboration improves student learning.

Their research shows schools with the highest level of collaboration, on average, have 12.5 percent more students performing at or above standards in English language arts and 4.5 percent more students at or above standards in math than schools with the lowest levels of collaboration, after adjusting for poverty (Alvarez and Rosales 2018).

In an online article by Rubinstein entitled "Strengthening Partnerships," he mentions educational reforms based on market forces (charter schools, vouchers, and high-stakes testing) take school improvement in the wrong direction. However, these ideas have dominated the policy debate in improving education. He says public schools must be examined for the way they are organized, the way decisions are made, and the way teaching and learning are improved.

Rubinstein is interested in the "product of democracy," "which means more democratic organizations, ones that value employees' voice and offer more decision-making opportunities, can be more productive." He has worked with unions and management in a variety of industries undergoing extensive changes due to globalization, including auto, steel, electronics communication, and now education.

His first experience with collaboration in public school education was in 1988 in Altoona, Pennsylvania. Through his years of consulting, Rubinstein noticed union leaders elected by members have a greater level of trust than nonelected management (Rubinstein 2013–2014).

In a November 29, 2018, webinar on YouTube entitled "National Labor Management Partnership: Collaborating for Student Success" (https://www.youtube.com/watch?v=pP3q9yDTOmM$feature=youtu.

CONCLUSION

be), the partners were the National Education Association (NEA), American Federation of Teachers (AFT), School Superintendents Association (AASA), and National School Boards Association (NSBA). Top officials from each organization spoke, as well as guest speaker Saul Rubinstein.

Rubinstein said the effects of collaboration in schools were higher student achievement including high-poverty school districts, improved commitment to education, and higher teacher retention including high-poverty schools. This was due to better quality (people closer to the problem were solving it) and better quantity (more resources were available).

Teachers were viewing their unions and administrations as a greater resource because they trusted them more due to collaboration. In traditional schools, the union role was for contract and grievance issues, primarily. With collaboration, the role was expanded to ensure educator voice in school and externally across the district via other union representatives. The collaboration was used for student performance data, mentoring, instructional practice, and curriculum development.

Mort Sherman, associate executive director for Leadership Network of AASA, spoke of beginning collaboration with shared goals. He said if all teachers collaborate, the students will collaborate with each other as well. Sherman mentioned the late Tom Sobol, an earlier advocate for transferring educational policy making from bureaucrats to educators and parents with his Compact for Learning. It did not work because it was a top-down mandate and not a collaborative mission. Also, there was little research at that point, as it preceded the research of Saul Rubinstein.

Randi Weingarten, president of AFT, said teachers have some of the highest levels of anxiety and stress levels across all professions. She noted with collaboration, teachers are not as stressed, and therefore, the students feel better. Her question was: how do we make collaboration the norm rather than the exception? Her recommendations were to share goals and create sustainable structures for local-level collaboration. They must be sustainable because if something goes wrong, you can bring it back. Structures mean building trust. You must talk to trust. Trust is earned among all stakeholders. It means being seen and being heard.

The climate is right for change now due to research and the current culture. Eighty percent of people want to strengthen education. Weingarten also said Betsy De Vos, former US secretary of education, wants to break the teacher unions, which is an example of the lack of collaboration at the federal level. Therefore, stakeholders must take more responsibility. The purpose of collaboration is all students succeed. Schools need to be safe and welcoming.

Becky Pringle, vice president of NEA at that time and now president of NEA, said shared leadership and shared decision-making must be at all levels. That means national, state, district, and school levels. It is not just about working together but building sustainable structures to sustain collaboration over time. This is a new era for leadership.

There is not one path for collaboration, but the common steps are: prepare the case for collaboration, act and implement collaboration with available resources from all levels, and reflect: Did the achievement match the intent? How does sustainable collaboration continue to improve and grow? The learning will come from teachers and parents, the ones closer to the students.

Tom Gentzel, recently retired executive director and CEO of NSBA, said stakeholders must collaborate internally and externally. He mentions new federal law says the local school leaders must take the lead because it is no longer the feds on down. The educational transformation must include the parents and the community because the public owns the schools because they fund and support education. The school board should represent public interests. Boards can establish policies for collaboration.

Keep the collaboration going. Establish a sustainable structure, so it is not diminished due to retirements and so forth. Engage with the business community around the skills gap: prepare students to enter the workforce in specific areas of need in their geographic area. For example, take a school that is located near a Tesla plant on a tour of the plant and invite guest speakers to speak of skills needed for their company now.

Jo Anderson, co-executive director of the Consortium for Educational Change (CEC), promotes collaborative labor-management relationships to systematically reform school districts and schools. At the district level, talk about what students need. At the state level, how do affiliates come together to support local work?

Andrea Walker, NEA associate director for Centers for Enterprise Strategy, said the way to save public education for the nation is through collaboration. Collaboration is not a new concept, but what is new is going beyond individuals to garner support by major groups to sustain it.

She recommended to start the collaboration conversation in schools. Additional resources are: the National Call to Action document, CEC's *Handbook for Collaboration*, NEA's *Collaborating for Student Success*, and the Center for American Progress article "Teacher Unions and Management Partnerships: How Working Together Improves Student Achievement" ("National Labor Management Partnership: Collaborating for Student Success" 2018).

Today there are more than 150 teacher-powered schools in at least twenty states from prekindergarten to age twenty-one. Prior to 2015, the majority were public charter schools due to more flexibility in organization, but since then, there has been a dramatic increase in the number of teacher-powered schools within traditional school districts. Sometimes teachers sign an agreement for collective autonomy with their district and teachers union. In a survey, 85 percent of Americans think teacher-powered schools are a good idea and 78 percent of teachers agree with that.

Teacher-led schools are not anti-principal: all these schools have administrators, but they work in collaboration with the teachers.

Some of the positives of a teacher-powered school are: When teachers know they are viewed as leaders, they act like leaders. They are collaborators with the administration and that builds trust between the two groups. There is less turnover of teachers, which means more continuity at the school. Collective decision-making creates more buy-in from the faculty and promotes a strong culture. More buy-in means the implementation will be more efficient. These schools are particularly good at producing deeper learning (Hodge 2019).

According to a 2017 study by Penn State University on teacher stress and health, teacher turnover leads to instability and lower effectiveness in US schools. Between 23 and 42 percent of teachers leave the profession within their first five years. Reasons include poor working conditions, low salary, student behavioral problems, and the lack of classroom resources, input into school-wide decision making, and supportive school leadership.

The National Commission on Teaching and America's Future estimates US schools are losing more than seven billion dollars each year in training new teachers when nearly half leave the profession within the first five years.

Teacher turnover usually occurs more frequently in poorly performing schools, which leads to long-term destabilization of low-income neighborhood schools who lose continuity in relationships between teachers, students, parents, and the community.

Teacher turnover results in lower student achievement. In a study of New York City fourth- and fifth-grade students with high teacher turnover, there was a significant negative effect on both math and language arts achievement. Turnover was especially harmful to lower-performing students (Greenberg, Brown, and Abenavoli 2016).

Teacher-led schools redefine school success as a holistic measure of student achievement beyond high-stakes testing. They prefer in-depth portfolios and comprehensive exams. They promote teacher voice, power, and leadership and strengthen teachers' commitment to the profession. These challenges keep teachers from boredom and complacency. Teachers go from feeling like industrial workers on a by-the-hour job who clock in and clock out to white-collar professionals in a partnership who own the firm.

According to a *Forbes* 2018 article entitled "The Teacher-Powered Schools Movement" (Langhorne 2018), schools with higher levels of teacher leadership produce greater student achievement. To attract well-qualified teachers, they will have to be offered professional status, compensation, and autonomy.

Teacher leadership is best when the teacher leaders are respected but not feared and they collaborate and nurture instead of punishing and enforcing. Teacher leaders like to share their knowledge with colleagues and the community. They need to be lifelong learners. But first and foremost, they earn the respect from colleagues, parents, and political leaders. The culture within the school must support teacher leaders. Everyone at the school is a problem solver—it is no longer your kids, but our kids.

The negatives of a teacher-led school include it takes more teacher work than traditional schools. However, teachers at these schools say it is more rewarding. Often, they delegate administrative tasks not related to direct contact with students to outside sources. For example, they might hire a bookkeeper. It is more difficult to implement and sustain with noncharter schools, as the traditional school has a more centralized system and is not as flexible. The mindset must shift to trust the teachers.

The change in leadership is the biggest challenge for noncharter schools. The loss of a supportive superintendent could endanger the teacher-powered schools. The appointment of a teacher leader by an administrator without other teacher input could contribute to conflict. For

CONCLUSION

example, other teachers might wonder, "Why you?" and "Why would you want to take it on?" Inadequate time for collaboration, learning, leading, and teaching could be an issue.

Also, cultural norms of distrust among teachers can be a problem if teachers want to be isolated and individual and not listen to their peer leader. In addition, traditional top-down leadership structures may get in the way (Langhorne 2018; The Center for Comprehensive School Reform and Improvement 2005; "Teacher Leadership: The Role of Educators in Our Schools and Communities" 2019).

How is a teacher-led school initiated? The Massachusetts Department of Elementary and Secondary Education's 2014–2015 Teacher and Principal Advisory Cabinets gave the following advice in a 2015 online article based on their collective experience. They said start with a current assessment of the collegial environment, problem-solving orientation, trust, and clear communication levels at the school against a checklist of questions by successful teacher-led schools.

For the collegial environment, do teachers collaborate before, after, and during school, informally and formally? Is there a shared vision among the faculty? ("Building a School Culture that Supports Teacher Leadership" 2015).

In an online article entitled "Teacher Collaboration: How to Approach It in 2020," author Lauren Davis, ed tech editor for Schoology Exchange and former department chair and instructional coach, mentions teacher collaboration is not only to learn from each other but also to share responsibility for all students' learning at that school. She defined collaboration as "purposely building interpersonal relationships and working towards healthy interdependence, which occurs when teachers are comfortable giving and receiving help without forfeiting accountability."

She says there are benefits when teachers coplan and coteach based on a shared vision. The benefits are increased academic effort, increased understanding of student data, more creative lesson plans, and less teacher isolation.

Increased academic effort occurs because collaborating teachers are all on the same page, so the level of academic rigor can be increased to match the core competencies they want the students to meet.

Increased understanding of student data from formative and summative assessments gives teachers a shared responsibility for celebrating success and analyzing failure.

More creative lesson plans result from an enlarged repertoire of instructional strategies from multiple teachers.

Less teacher isolation improves staff morale and professional satisfaction.

Lauren Davis writes many schools are inconsistent or unstructured in their approach to highly effective teacher collaboration. She mentions the most common challenges to it are lack of a true Professional Learning Community (PLC), lack of planning, lack of collaboration or reflection time, and personality conflicts and territoriality.

There must be a formal and regular commitment to PLCs or teacher collaboration will not happen across the school. The power of it diminishes, and teachers view it as optional and just another meaningless thing on their plate. PLCs have a direct influence on student engagement and achievement, as well as growth for the educators within them.

Develop and agree upon a shared vision and mutual goals, so teachers buy into it and feel a sense of pride and ownership. For example, if a team is committed to building relationships with students, set goals related to that vision, discuss how to reach those goals, and assess the progress regularly.

PLCs take time to develop, and a sense of community within the group must be established. Take the time to get to know your colleagues on a personal as well as professional level. When technology is part of the PLC, the online knowledge, experience, and resources of outside educators can provide more collaboration, including video technology like Zoom or Google Hangouts.

There must be common planning time for teachers embedded into the workday so they can collaborate and reflect together.

Collaborative groups will be composed of different personalities and viewpoints. It is a good idea to establish norms, have a conflict management plan, monitor one's emotions, and always use professional judgment.

For the problem-solving orientation, is the staff more interested in solving problems than complaining about them? Are the students a shared responsibility? Do the students' successes and challenges belong to everyone?

For the trust component, is everyone focused on mutual growth and improvement? Do staff feel their concerns are heard before everyone rallies around a solution? With a top-down leadership, solutions are decided by the administration and teachers are expected to follow through, regardless if they agree with them or not.

For clear communication, are there clear, predictable, and reliable communication structures in place, such as weekly e-mail updates or monthly staff meetings? Is there two-way communication between teachers and administrators? Do the administrators only tell teachers what to do instead of asking questions and seeking answers from the teachers? Can teachers initiate the questions to the administrators? Does everyone feel "in the loop" and on the same page communication-wise or is communication only with select groups? (Davis 2020).

Administrators need to ask themselves if they are honestly ready for teacher leaders with the following questions:

1. Do I know all my teachers' individual talents and interests well? If not, send out a survey to gauge teachers' interests and talents in areas like data analysis, technology, education policy, public speaking, and so on. These talents could be used to the school community's advantage. Give everyone the opportunity to lead. Acknowledge teachers who already take on informal leadership roles and ask how you can support them ("Building a School Culture that Supports Teacher Leadership" 2015).

    A 2017 online article entitled "How Should Administrators Empower Teacher Collaboration?" suggests that administrators could model future teacher teams after something the teachers are familiar with: PLCs. Typically, a teacher team would have one leader and several other educators with varying levels of responsibilities working to meet student needs (Chatlani 2017).
2. What are the real nonnegotiables? Share with teachers the areas you will not allow them to lead in, for example, school safety. If you are upfront with boundaries, teachers will respect your limits.
3. Does "handing over the reins" make me feel like I am losing control? Reflect on why that is and identify a small starter project that you feel safe letting go of. Being a principal is an enormous job. Be aware of your own strengths and weaknesses and where you could use help. If you are open and honest with teachers, there is a better chance they will trust and want to help you.

    Use the start of the new school year or a staff meeting to communicate your deliberate intent of teacher leadership and why it is important to school culture and staff morale. Talk about how you want to implement it ("Building a School Culture that Supports Teacher Leadership" 2015).

John Maxwell's book *The 360 Degree Leader* has multiple leadership methods that can be applied to help administrators, not only to benefit student outcomes but also to improve relationships with their teachers that can help with teacher retention.

One method, called leading up, features empowering teachers with more opportunities so they become better leaders, instead of undermining their decision making. A second method, leading horizontally, means administrators expand a project adding a teacher component, to build trust with their teachers; for example, offering the teachers a chance to conduct case studies that analyze student outcomes. A third method, leading downward, is when administrators offer tips to teachers on topics like data collection, so they can begin to become decision makers.

At the 2017 Education Commission for the States National Forum on Education Policy, many educators said they frequently could not get involved in administrative meetings because they happened when they were teaching in the classroom. Moving administrative meetings to a time outside of the teacher workday can improve the school climate for educators (Chatlani 2017).

4. How do teachers go about sharing ideas with me? When teachers raise a concern, am I comfortable listening or do I mentally prepare my response before they are finished? Principals who leave their door physically open during the day, except for private meetings, have a more welcoming mindset for the school. When there is a meeting, they sit at a table next to their teachers away from their desk and give their full attention. They take notes and have eye contact with their teachers. When they say they will get back to their teachers, they really do.

Regardless of a school's culture and the openness of the principal or one's colleagues, teachers need to have a voice in their profession, whether it is formal or informal. Teachers can take small steps to improve their school's culture. They can collaborate more with other teachers through projects, observations, and going to trainings together. Teachers can approach their principals with not just problems but ideas with solutions to problems and seek the principal's input on this.

Do not avoid leadership because of fear of failure because then the environment of empowered teacher leaders will never exist. If teachers take chances outside of their comfort zone, it may encourage other teachers and administrators to do so as well.

Teachers need to see themselves as leaders now. They do not need to be anointed with superpowers. What is a problem at your school that you want to solve? Ask questions to understand why the problem exists. What small steps can you take to get you started? How have you impacted your school beyond the classroom?

Just be careful not to burn yourself out. You need to find allies. There is support in numbers. Find people who are interested in the problem you want to solve. Brainstorm with them possible solutions. Ask your principal directly how they feel about teacher leadership. If they are on board, collaborate with your administration to solve these problems ("Building a School Culture that Supports Teacher Leadership" 2015).

A district that has incorporated collaboration since 2004 is ABC Unified School District in Los Cerritos (a suburb outside of Los Angeles), California. Typically, the change to collaboration is due to a crisis to motivate a change in union-management relations.

ABC District was no exception: in the early 1990s, it went on strike for eight days over budget concerns and the district's plan to slash teachers' health benefits and pay while increasing class size. When the strike was settled, the result was an educational partnership between the union and the district. The partnership was the most effective way to improve teacher quality and student performance.

The union and the district abide by six guiding principles:

1. All students can succeed, and we will not accept any excuse that prevents that from happening at ABC. We will work together to promote student success.
2. All needed support will be made available to schools to ensure every student succeeds. We will work together to ensure that happens.
3. The top 5 percent of teachers in our profession should teach our students. We will together hire, train, and retain these professionals.

4. All employees contribute to student success.
5. All negotiations support conditions that sustain successful teaching and student learning.
6. We will not let each other fail. A mantra at the ABC School District is: We work to solve problems and not to win arguments.

This school served as the basis for research by Rubinstein and McCarthy on their report "How Working Together Improves Student Achievement." This collaboration of teachers, administration, and the teacher union has survived multiple superintendents and several school board elections.

It has led to a district culture of "shared planning, decision-making, and responsibility" that is "built on respect, commitment, and trust." The teachers and administration have worked together on curriculum development, textbook selection, recruitment and hiring, mentoring, teacher evaluation and support, and use of data-based decision making (O'Brien 2014).

At the university level, it is encouraging to see recent education majors connecting with stakeholders and getting a taste of reality before they step into the classroom. At the University of Nevada, Reno, students call retired or current educators playing the role of "parents" to learn how to communicate with parents.

Also, guest speakers, current or retired teachers, talk with students about how to build relationships with their stakeholders. These education majors recently made a list of the questions they are most worried about in their future careers. It was submitted and answered by retired and current teachers in the district.

Some student questions and answers by educators were:

1. How do teachers remember everything they want to say without having a notecard or script in front of them?

Teachers do not remember everything. They might have an outline of the lesson in front of them as well as on the board or projector for the students to follow.

2. What is the best way to separate work and home life in a career where it is so easy to take it home and let it affect you after the fact or spill over into home? Especially in the current circumstances of distance learning due to COVID-19.

The best way is to establish a clear boundary. When at work, finish the work and make all the necessary contacts. Put the next day's lesson plan outline on the board and close the door and your school world. When at home, do not work on schoolwork, nor check your e-mails nor return communications. Any school-related items that make it home, like a school bag, are not allowed in the bedroom.

If a husband and wife are both teachers, at home try to limit school talk and put your concentration on your families and your hobbies. During COVID-19, if you have a second bedroom or guest room, treat it like your classroom at school. Be there during required school hours. Set preparation time but close the door and leave that world after that.

3. What are effective ways to deescalate tension between yourself, students, parents, other teachers, and the administration?

First, thank the other person for getting together with you to solve an issue together. Ask them, "How can I help you?" Then sit back and really listen.

4. How do teachers deal with getting behind in their lesson plans? For example, if a lesson is derailed by an assembly or classroom disturbance, what can teachers do to get the classroom back up to speed?

Look through the lesson and see if any of it can be cut. If not, and you teach other classes with the same lesson and you do not want to get out of sequence, slow down other classes and review with them or give them an activity that applies the concepts you are teaching to the class that got behind.

5. What are effective ways to incentivize students to turn their missing work in late? Some students think that, "Hey, it's late one day, might as well not do it at all." How do we change this?

Do not accept assignments late except for excused absences or excused tardiness. With this clear boundary stated in your syllabus, you will not have issues with late homework and will have a high turn-in rate. If a student is not doing their homework, contact their parents and write a summary afterward of the conversation in a communication log you set up. This log should include the student and the parent names, their phone number or e-mail address, the date, and the nature of the contact. If there is a parent-teacher meeting down the road, you could show evidence you had previously contacted the parent.

You could also ask the student why they are not doing their homework. Based on their answer, you might negotiate, accepting half of their assignments to get them back on track, but after that, they have to follow the rules of the class so as not to show favoritism to one student.

6. When do teachers plan to individually meet with students?

Set up office hours and post them outside your classroom door. Have students sign up in a binder ahead of time with the date, what class period they are from, and what they need help with. That way you can have the necessary materials ready. Limit the number of students to maybe five and warn them they must bring other work as you make your way around the classroom to help everyone. Expect them to come to you with specific questions and put effort into the assignment. It is not your job to do their homework for them.

During a parent-teacher conference, you can use the binder to reference how often the student has come in for extra help.

7. What is most important to know before student teaching? Do you just walk in on the first day and take over for the lead teacher, or are you eased into the classroom?

The most important thing to know before student teaching is to make sure you have a mentor teacher who is positive and someone you can trust, especially at times when you feel vulnerable due to your inexperience. You must be reliable, see this as a job, and be on time with your deadlines. The mentor teacher is there to guide you but not there to do your work for you.

Interning is a gradual process. You begin as the observer, and then gradually transition to assisting the teacher, coteaching with the teacher, and finally taking over the classroom. Never take over for the lead teacher on the first day.

8. How do teachers make time to get to know their students on a personal level that may not have to do with academics?

Have the students fill out index cards on the first day of school answering questions about their interests and goals in life. Read over these cards. When you greet them at the door or after class or during office hours, talk to them about what they wrote on the cards. It shows you care about them as more than a student.

9. How do teachers manage all the aspects of teaching—lesson planning, grading, classroom management, etc.?

The management becomes easier as you become a seasoned teacher. In the beginning, lesson plan one week in advance, grade and post immediately, and set firm rules and follow through right away for consistency.

CONCLUSION

10. When do teachers know when the content they teach or the delivery of the instruction becomes too difficult for their students?

Teachers know by constantly assessing their students informally and formally. Watch their facial expressions during a lecture. When you give a classroom assignment, peer over the students' shoulders and see how they are doing. Listen in on group work. Call on students randomly in class. Give out regular homework. Tests of course will give major feedback, but you want to know where they are long before the test, so you can reteach difficult concepts if necessary.

11. What are your favorite classroom management strategies?

Have a mantra and live by it. For example, "Every child has the right to learn." This supersedes everything. Do not tolerate bullying nor distractions interfering with student learning. Tell students at the beginning of the year your mantra, and warn them that if you change their seats and they ask you why, you will repeat your mantra.

Make sure you can get to any student at any time by insisting on clear aisles and walking the room constantly. You want that individual connection with your students.

12. When do teachers decide to stop grading for the day? Do they stay after school ends and grade while they are on campus, or do they only grade after school from home? Is it a mix of both?

Teachers adopt strategies that work for them. For example, some do not leave school until their assignments for that day are graded and posted. If there is a project, they might give themselves a week to grade and post it. Try not to grade from home during the week; although sometimes on the weekends, you might need to grade lengthier tests. The main thing is to not get behind in grading because students need immediate feedback, you will get less parent phone calls, and it keeps your stress level down.

13. What are effective ways to encourage distracted/uninterested learners to participate in class?

Do not be afraid to call on them! Use the index cards mentioned previously in question 8 to call randomly on students. Randomly keeps student on their toes. Feel free to constantly shuffle the pile and repeatedly call on students.

Talk to distracted/uninterested students privately and find out what is going on. If they are unreceptive, call their parents and talk with their guidance counselor. Do not give up on them.

14. What is important to know for interacting with a principal or dean? How do you get on their good side?

You must be a team player and follow the school rules. Being disrespectful to your administration will put you on their bad side. Being late to a faculty meeting and making a grand entrance is not a good idea. You must be on time with all deadlines. It is not fair that you hold up a school project that everyone else has bought into.

15. When and how do teachers do their lesson planning? How far in advance? 180 days need to be lesson planned?

Veteran teachers save lesson plans from year to year if they teach the same class and update and reuse them. For new teachers or teachers teaching a new subject, have your large unit outlines planned out over the summer, but day-to-day lessons can be planned one week in advance. Do not get too far in front, as you will be adjusting as you go along.

16. How do teachers discuss student progress with families? How do teachers discuss their curriculum needs to their administrator?

Teachers discuss student progress with families for secondary education at prearranged parent-teacher meetings. At the elementary level, they are often planned as conference weeks where all parents meet with teachers at preassigned times.

At the beginning of the year, teachers have preevaluation conferences with their administrators. That is a great time to discuss curriculum needs. The rest of the year, e-mail your school secretary, who is often in charge of meetings with the principal, and schedule a meeting to speak with them. Never drop in on a principal for a meeting. It is fine if their door is open to just say, "Hi," but it is rude to expect them to drop everything to fit you in.

17. When do teachers receive reviews/feedback from the administration, and how often?

Reviews and feedback frequency vary depending upon the teacher's status. A new teacher will have more frequent reviews. A teacher who has had multiple complaints from parents or students will have more frequent reviews as well. Reviews are scheduled with pre and post conferences.

Some schools have a walk-through system, where the administrator will randomly walk through classrooms unannounced and leave short feedback for the teacher.

CONCLUSION

18. What are effective ways to encourage shy or quiet students to ask a question? How are teachers able to tell if they are understanding the content?

Talk with shy students informally at the door to build a connection. During a class discussion, ask them what they think. Invite them into the conversation. As you walk the room, look over their shoulder and see how they are doing. Observe how they are doing when you put them into a group.

19. How do teachers analyze their assessments and make changes to their upcoming lesson plans effectively in a short time?

Teachers should always reflect on the lesson they just taught. Write directly underneath the lesson plan what went well and what did not and why. Adjust immediately if you are teaching the same lesson again later that day.

Analyze your assessments using a preestablished rubric. By the way, give the students the rubric before assigning the project. They will do a better job the more specific you are in your rubric.

20. Logistically it sems like a dumpster fire of a mess especially with ever-changing curriculum, classes, standards, and your own style.

It may seem that way, but once you start teaching, you will see that changes occur gradually. You can keep your own style within the standards. They may dictate what you teach but not how you teach it. The curriculum may change, but often you can adapt your previous lesson plans to fit into the changes. Just remember, you are teaching students and not curriculum. Your priority is to connect with them, and the rest will follow.

These current and future educators have questions that need answers. They need to dare and take the time to establish connections with their stakeholders: other teachers, their students, the students' parents, administrators, and the community because that establishes them as a professional teacher, someone the stakeholders can trust and work with.

BIBLIOGRAPHY

Adams, Caralee. "15 Smart Ways to Fight Teacher Burnout That Really Work." We Are Teachers (blog), December 5, 2019. https://www.weareteachers.com/prevent-teacher-burnout/.

Alber, Rebecca. "A Phone Call Home Makes All of the Difference." Edutopia, August 24, 2017. https://www.edutopia.org/article/phone-call-home-makes-all-difference.

Alvarez, Brenda. 2015. "Teacher-Led Schools: They Are Here, and More Are on the Way." *NEA Today*, February 12, 2015. https://www.nea.org/advocating-for-change/new-from-nea/teacher-led-schools-theyre-here-and-more-are-way.

Alvarez, Brenda, and Rosales, John. "The Case for Collaboration is Clear." *NEA Today*, December 4, 2018. https://www.nea.org/advocating-for-change/new-from-nea/case-collaboration-clear.

Anderson, Melinda. 2016. "How Discrimination Shapes Parent-Teacher Communication." *The Atlantic*, November 15, 2016. https://www.theatlantic.com/education/archive/2016/11/which-parents-are-teachers-most-likely-to-contact/507755/.

Assembly Bill (AB) 521. Nevada State Education Association, 1998. https://ccea-nv.org/images/stories/pdfs/Forms/ab521.pdf.

Babones, Salvatore. "Education "Reform's Big Lie: The Real Reason the Right Has Declared War on Our Public Schools." *Salon*, May 9, 2015. https://www.salon.com/2015/05/09/education_reforms_big_lie_the_real_reason_the_right_has_declared_war_on_our_public_schools/.

Banks, James. "Diversity, Group Identity, and Citizenship Education in a Global Age." *Educational Researcher* 37, no. 3 (April 2008): 129–139.

Bennett, Nneka A. "6 Ways to Prevent Racism in Schools." Kickboard (blog), July 6, 2018. https://www.kickboardforschools.com/blog/post/diversity-equity/6-ways-to-prevent-racism-in-schools/.

Berdan, Stacie. "What Does Language Proficiency Mean?" 2020. https://stacieberdan.com/what-does-language-proficiency-mean/.

Brown, Brené. *Daring Greatly: How the Courage to Be Vulnerable Transforms the Way We Live, Love, Parent, and Lead*. New York: Avery, 2012.

"Building a School Culture that Supports Teacher Leadership." Massachusetts Department of Elementary and Secondary Education, July 2015. https://www.doe.mass.edu/edeffectiveness/leadership/building-school-culture.pdf.

Burton, Jonathan. "You're Probably Not Ready to Retire—Psychologically." *MarketWatch*, August 4, 2019. https://www.marketwatch.com/story/why-youre-probably-not-psychologically-ready-to-retire-2019-05-21.

BIBLIOGRAPHY

The Center for Comprehensive School Reform and Improvement. "What Does the Research Tell Us about Teacher Leadership?" Reading Rockets, 2005. https://www.readingrockets.org/article/what-does-research-tell-us-about-teacher-leadership.

Chan, Justin. "Teacher Resigns in front of School Board, Delivers Powerful Message to Students in Viral Video." *Yahoo! Sports*, February 25, 2020. https://sports.yahoo.com/2020-02-25-teacher-resigns-in-front-of-school-board-delivers-powerful-message-to-students-in-viral-video-23934100.html.

Chatlani, Shalina. "How Should Administrators Empower Teacher Collaboration?" *Education Dive*, July 6, 2017. https://www.educationdive.com/news/administrators-enhance-collaboration-teachers/446401/.

"Combating Racism and Discrimination in and through Education." European Commission Against Racism and Intolerance (ECRI), 2019. https://rm.coe.int/ecri-general-policy-recommendation-no-10-key-topics-combating-racism-a/16808b75f7.

Corwin, Sylvie. "Student Voices: Why I need timely feedback from my teachers." *Seattle Times* Education Lab, April 22, 2016. https://www.seattletimes.com/education-lab/student-voices-why-i-need-more-feedback-from-my-teachers/.

Davis, Lauren. "Teacher Collaboration: How to Approach It in 2020." Schoology Exchange (blog), February 1, 2020. https://www.schoology.com/blog/teacher-collaboration.

Dempsey, Tom. "Teachers Relieved After State Ruling in SMSD Contract Dispute." *KSHB TV News*, February 15, 2020. https://www.kshb.com/news/local-news/teachers-relieved-after-state-ruling-in-smsd-contract-dispute.

Empower Nevada Teachers. 2019. https://empowernvteachers.org/.

FindLaw Team of Legal Writers and Editors. 2016. "Teachers' Unions and Collective Bargaining: Overview." FindLaw, June 20, 2016. https://www.findlaw.com/education/teachers-rights/teachers-unions-and-collective-bargaining-overview.html.

Finholm, Valerie. "You're Boss and Don't Let Kids Forget It." *The Hartford Courant*, March 16, 1996. https://www.courant.com/news/connecticut/hc-xpm-1996-03-16-9603160052-story.html.

Fink, Jennifer. "Teacher Depression and Anxiety Are So Common. Here's How to Cope." We Are Teachers (blog), April 18, 2018. https://www.weareteachers.com/teacher-depression-anxiety/.

Finley, Todd. "Mastering Classroom Transitions." Edutopia, March 13, 2017. https://www.edutopia.org/article/mastering-transitions-todd-finley.

French, J. R. P., and B. Raven. "The Bases of Social Power." In *Group Dynamics: Research and Theory*, edited by D. Cartwright and A. Zander, 607–623. Evanston, IL: Row-Peterson, 1960.

Gerhardt-Cooper, Tracy. 2019. "Empowering Kids Will Take Them Further Than Enabling." *The Ascent*, November 11, 2019. https://medium.com/the-ascent/empowering-kids-will-take-them-further-than-enabling-2014ac45bc1e.

"Getting Started with Peer Observation." *Cambridge Assessment International Education*, 2005. https://www.cambridge-community.org.uk/professional-development/gswpo/index.html.

Ginsburg, David. "Education Reform Key: Stop Enabling Students' Self-Defeating Behavior." *Education Week*, February 13, 2011. https://blogs.edweek.org/teachers/coach_gs_teaching_tips/2011/02/education_reform_key_stop_enabling_students_self-defeating_behavior.html.

Glink, Steven E. "Teacher Rights." Education Rights, 2018. https://www.educationrights.com/teacherrights.php.

Goldstein, Dana, and Erica Green. "What the Supreme Court's Janus Decision Means for Teacher Unions." *The New York Times*, June 27, 2018. https://www.nytimes.com/2018/06/27/us/teacher-unions-fallout-supreme-court-janus.html.

Greenberg, M. T., J. L. Brown, and R. M. Abenavoli. "Teacher Stress and Health." Pennsylvania State University, September 1, 2016. https://www.rwjf.org/en/library/research/2016/07/teacher-stress-and-health.html.

Grossenbacher, John. "Rebuilding Public Education is Essential to Saving America." *The Hill*, February 28, 2019. https://thehill.com/opinion/education/431087-rebuilding-public-education-is-essential-to-saving-america.

Guskey, Thomas R., and Associates. "Solving the Problems of Zeros in Grading." June 25, 2013. http://tguskey.com/solving-problems-zeros-grading/.

Haigler, Adam. "When Teachers Run the School: The Francine Delany Story." Teacher-Powered Schools, April 26, 2018. https://www.teacherpowered.org/blog/when-teachers-run-school-francine-delany-story.

Hodge, Maggie. "How School Leaders Can Empower Every Teacher to be a Leader on Campus." *Education Elements*, May 22, 2019. https://www.edelements.com/blog/how-school-leaders-can-empower-every-teacher-to-be-a-leader-on-campus#:~:text=A%20focus%20on%20key%20leadership,leaders%2C%20they%20a.

Jackson, Sam. "Female Professors Receive More Work Demands." *The Easterner*, April 30, 2019. https://theeasterner.org/45957/arts-entertainment-features/female-professors-get-greater-work-demands-ewu-study-says/.

Kamb, Rachel. "Key Factors in Creating a Positive Classroom Climate." Committee for Children (blog), August 12, 2012. https://www.cfchildren.org/blog/2012/08/key-factors-in-creating-a-positive-classroom-climate/.

Kelly, Melissa. "Are Teachers Required to Join Teacher Unions?" *ThoughtCo*, March 14, 2020. https://www.thoughtco.com/are-teachers-required-to-join-teacher-unions-8382#:~:text=While%20union%20membership%20is%20not,unions%20pay%20their%20teachers%20more.%E2%80%9D.

Klein, Alissa, and Christian Moriarty. "You're Funnier than You Think: Using Humor in the Classroom." *Faculty Focus*, November 13, 2017. https://www.facultyfocus.com/articles/effective-teaching-strategies/using-humor-classroom/.

Knight, Anamaria. "How to Prepare Globally Competent Students." *Medium*, March 3, 2016. https://medium.com/@anamaria.knight/how-to-prepare-globally-competent-students-92d805d13fdd.

Lam, Kristin. "Teachers' Failure to Update Grades Raises Concerns." *The Bruin Voice*, February 4, 2015. https://bruinvoice.net/1885/news/teachers-failure-to-update-grades-raises-concerns/.

Landfried, Steven E. "Educational Enabling: Is "Helping" Hurting Our Students?" *Middle School Journal* 21, no. 5 (1990): 12–15. http://www.jstor.org/stable/23023804.

———. "Enabling" Undermines Responsibility in Students." *Educational Leadership,* November 1989. http://www.ascd.org/ASCD/pdf/journals/ed_lead/el_198911_landfried.pdf.

Langhorne, Emily. "The Teacher-Powered Schools Movement: Transforming Teachers from Industrial Workers to Professionals." *Forbes*, July 11, 2018. https://www.forbes.com/sites/emilylanghorne/2018/07/11/the-teacher-powered-schools-movement-transforming-teachers-from-industrial-workers-to-professionals/?sh=200937b87da1.

"Lesson Plan Self-Reflection and Evaluation." St. Teresa of Avila Catholic Student Center at Valparaiso University, September 2017. https://saintt.com/documents/2017/9/LessonPlanReflectionAssessment.pdf.

Manno, Bruno V. "Teacher-Powered Schools Are Putting Educators in the Driver's Seat." *Washington Examiner*, July 28, 2019. https://www.washingtonexaminer.com/opinion/op-eds/teacher-powered-schools-are-putting-educators-in-the-drivers-seat.

Maxwell, John. *The 360 Degree Leader: Developing Your Influence from Anywhere in the Organization*. New York: HarperCollins, 2006.

Meador, Derrick. "Pros and Cons of Joining a Teachers Union." *ThoughtCo,* January 6, 2019. https://www.thoughtco.com/weighing-the-decision-to-join-a-teachers-union-3194787.

Minero, Emelina. "Do No-Zero Policies Help or Hurt Students?" Edutopia, July 3, 2018. https://www.edutopia.org/article/do-no-zero-policies-help-or-hurt-students.

Morin, Amy. 2016. "There is a Clear Line Between Oversharing and Being Authentic—Here's How to Avoid Crossing It." *Forbes*, October 22, 2016. https://www.forbes.com/sites/amymorin/2016/10/22/there-is-a-clear-line-between-oversharing-and-being-authentic-heres-how-to-avoid-crossing-it/?sh=1b7ef20d56e3.

Moxley, Elle. "The Kansas Labor Secretary Sides with Shawnee Mission Teachers, Overturns District's Contract." KCUR 89.3, February 14, 2020. https://www.kcur.org/education/2020-02-14/the-kansas-labor-secretary-sides-with-shawnee-mission-teachers-overturns-districts-contract.

"National Labor Management Partnership: Collaborating for Student Success." YouTube. National Education Association, November 29, 2018. https://www.youtube.com/watch?v=pP3q9yDTOmM.

O'Brien, Anne. 2014. "When Teachers and Administrators Collaborate." Edutopia, November 20, 2014. https://www.edutopia.org/blog/when-teachers-and-administrators-collaborate-anne-obrien.

Parsons, Ginna. "John Rosemond: Research Clear: Obedient Children Are Happy Children." *Daily Journal*, February 16, 2020. https://www.djournal.com/lifestyle/john-rosemond-research-clear-obedient-children-are-happy-children/article_6db1cf08-ff3b-57f9-9441-734db2f80e1b.html.

Participate Learning. "7 Shocking Statistics Illustrating the Importance of Global Education." 2016. *Medium*, February 22, 2016. https://medium.com/global-perspectives/7-shocking-statistics-illustrating-the-importance-of-global-education-b6b68d70e22d.

Paul, Michael. "3 Ways to Reflect with Purpose." Edutopia, May 10, 2016. https://www.edutopia.org/discussion/3-ways-reflect-purpose.

Ravitch, Diane. "Standardized Testing Undermines Teaching." *Fresh Air*, NPR, April 28, 2011. https://www.npr.org/2011/04/28/135142895/ravitch-standardized-testing-undermines-teaching#:~:text=Diane%20Ravitch%3A%20Standardized%20Testing%20Undermines%20Teaching%20%3A%20NPR&text=Diane%20Ravitch%3A%20Standardized%20Testing%20Undermines%20Teaching%20Former%20Assistant%20Secretary%20of,and%20what%20changed%20her%20mind.

Renard, Lucie. "How to Become a Reflective Teacher-The Complete Guide for Reflection in Teaching." Book Widgets (blog), February 21, 2019. https://www.bookwidgets.com/blog/2019/02/how-to-become-a-reflective-teacher-the-complete-guide-for-reflection-in-teaching.

Rosemond, John. "Parenting Advice with John Rosemond: New Way of Parenting Hyper Focused on Kids' Feelings." *Statesboro Herald*, October 1, 2016. https://www.statesboroherald.com/life/parenting-advice-with-john-rosemond-new-way-of-parenting-hyperfocused-on-kids-feelings/.

———. 2018. "Teachers Lack Support from Parents." *Gaston Gazette*, August 23, 2018. https://www.gastongazette.com/entertainmentlife/20180823/john-rosemond-teachers-lack-support-from-parents.

Ross, Tamie. "Standing Firm, John Rosemond Talks About Parents, Kids and Discipline." *The Oklahoman*, March 8, 1998. https://oklahoman.com/article/2605304/standing-firm-john-rosemond-talks-about-parents-kids-and-discipline.

Rubinstein, Saul. "Strengthening Partnerships: How Communication and Collaboration Contribute to School Improvement." *American Educator* (Winter 2013–2014): 22–28. https://www.aft.org/sites/default/files/periodicals/Rubinstein.pdf.

Ryshke, Robert. "What's the Value of Homework and Should It Be Graded?" Center for Teaching, September 4, 2011. https://rryshke.org/2011/09/04/whats-the-value-of-homework-and-should-it-be-graded/.

Salazar, Ray. "Why I Still Give My Students Zeros." National Board for Professional Teaching Standards, April 4, 2019. https://www.nbpts.org/why-i-still-give-my-students-zeros/#:~:text=So%2C%20yes%2C%20students%20can%20earn,t%20do%20every%20single%20assignment.&text=In%20fact%2C%20giving%20zeros%20for,can't%20do%20it%20all.

Sands, Bill. "How Open Should You Be with Your Students About Your Personal Life?" Study.com, November 2017. https://study.com/blog/how-open-should-you-be-with-your-students-about-your-personal-life.html.

Segaren, Sharuna. "The Importance of Diversity in Education Faculties." *Study International*, March 18, 2019. https://www.studyinternational.com/news/the-importance-of-diversity-in-education-faculties/.

Shindler, John. "Transformative Classroom Management Resource Site." California State University, Los Angeles, 2018. http://web.calstatela.edu/faculty/jshindl/cm/.

Soper, Sheldon. "The Implications of Grading Without Zeros." Teach.Com, January 16, 2018. https://teach.com/blog/grading-without-zeros/.

"Social Isolation, Loneliness in Older People Pose Health Risks." National Institute on Aging, April 23, 2019. https://www.nia.nih.gov/news/social-isolation-loneliness-older-people-pose-health-risks#:~:text=Research%20has%20linked%20social%20isolation,Alzheimer's%20disease%2C%20and%20even%20death.

Speer, Carolyn. "Establishing Authority in Your Classroom." Wichita State University, 2017. https://www.wichita.edu/services/mrc/instructional_technology/Pedagogy/EstablishingClassroomAuthority.php.

Stanley, Caroline M. "Consulting a Clown." *Inside Higher Ed*, November 28, 2017. https://www.insidehighered.com/advice/2017/11/28/importance-using-humor-classroom-essay.

Stark, Katherine. 2019. "Reevaluating the Importance of Foreign Languages." *The Current*, November 24, 2019. https://thecurrentmsu.com/2019/11/24/reevaluating-the-importance-of-foreign-languages/.

Stearns, Clio, and Leslie Chapel. "Using Humor in the Classroom." Study.com, n.d. https://study.com/academy/lesson/using-humor-in-the-classroom.html.

"Teacher Leadership: The Role of Educators in Our Schools and Communities." Campbellsville University, July 11, 2019. https://online.campbellsville.edu/education/teacher-leadership/#:~:text=Teacher%20leaders%20are%20in%20the,practices%20and%20increase%20student%20achievement.

Teacher-Powered Schools. "About the Movement." 2020. https://www.teacherpowered.org/about.

"Teaching Global Competence." Edutopia, January 30, 2013. https://www.edutopia.org/stw-global-competence-classroom-tips-video.

"There's a Reason Tenure Cannot Be Taken from a Nevada Public School Teacher, and It's Simple." *Desert Beacon*, March 19, 2015. https://desertbeacon.wordpress.com/2015/03/19/theres-a-reason-tenure-cannot-be-taken-from-a-nevada-public-school-teacher-and-its-simple/.

Vagins, Deborah J. "Is Race Discrimination in School Discipline a Real Problem?" ACLU, January 8, 2014. https://www.aclu.org/blog/racial-justice/race-and-inequality-education/race-discrimination-school-discipline-real-problem.

Vandenberg, Jenna. "Why Homework Matters: It's Not Just About Grades." *Parent Map*, April 16, 2019. https://www.parentmap.com/article/why-homework-matters-its-not-just-about-grades.

Washoe Education Association (WEA). 2020. http://www.weatoday.org/.

Young, David. "Global Education for Every Student." *SEEN*, November 23, 2014. https://www.seenmagazine.us/Articles/Article-Detail/ArticleId/4387/GLOBAL-EDUCATION-FOR-EVERY-STUDENT.

———. "What Do Globally Competent Students Look Like?" Getting Smart, February 23, 2016. https://www.gettingsmart.com/2016/02/what-do-globally-competent-students-look-like/.

"Your Educator Association Rights." TeacherFreedom.org, 2020. https://teacherfreedom.org/educator-association-rights/.

Zelinski, Ernie. *How to Retire Happy, Wild, and Free: Retirement Wisdom that You Won't Get from Your Financial Advisor.* Edmonton, Canada: Visions International, 2009.

INDEX

anxiety and depression: reducing, 72–73, 129; retirement related, 112, 119–120; school related, 78–79
assessments: authentic, 9; common, 43; informal, formal, 141; method of, 12–13; rubric for, 19, 143

bullying: parent to teacher, 58–59; student to student, 6, 70, 141; student to teacher, 58–59, 94; teacher to student, 35
burnout, xi–xii; retirement related, 113; school related, 42, 69; teacher leadership related, 137

cheating, 16, 62
child protective services, 105
classroom climate, 51–52
classroom management, 140, 141; at the door, 3; cell phone policy, 4, 38; establish authority, 53–59; establish credibility, 7; transitions, 13–15
classroom routines, 5, 49; absent student, 9; bathroom policy, 38–39; clear aisles, 5, 141; consistency, 49; dismissal, 6; starting class, 5
classroom spending, 70
communication with administration: teacher administrator meeting, 48, 142
communication with parents: parent teacher meeting, 46–47, 48–49, 139, 142; phone call or email to home, 34–35, 46–49, 138
connection to students, 143; empathy, 5; index cards, 52, 140, 141; moving around classroom, 5; pronouncing names correctly, 5

death: relative, 60–61; student, 105–106
discipline: progressive discipline plan, 95–97; racial bias, 34–36
dress code, 41

education reform, 23, 95, 98–99, 128
effective classroom observation(eco). *See* reflection of others
enabling vs. helping, 61–68; academic enabling, 62–63; behavioral enabling, 62–64; codependency, 64, 69; consequences of, 64, 67; reducing enabling, 64–66
entitled students, 21, 42
expectations of female vs. male teachers, 42, 53–54
extra credit, 62, 70

faculty: importance of diverse, 33–34
federal government: involvement in education, 98–99
fifteenth year in, 50
foreign language. *See* world language

INDEX

friendship with students: online, 50; post-graduation, 50

future of education, 127–138; ABC District, 137–138; administrator's role, 131, 135–138; collaboration, xii, 128–131, 133–138; professional learning community, 134–135; teacher-led or teacher-powered schools, 127–128, 131–133

global citizens, 25, 29

global competence, ix; definition of, 24; proficiency in a foreign language, 24–25, 27

global education, 24–37; access to, 27–28; benefits of, 25–27; cultural diversity, 33–34; culturally relevant teaching, 8, 35–36; curiosity, 26, 29, 72; definition of, 24; educate against racism, 33; implementation of, 27, 29–31, 37; McQueen High School, 28–29; necessity of, ix; promote global education, 8; racial bias, 34–37; racism definition, 36; resources, 31, 33; Teachers for Global Classrooms (TGC), 31, 37; teaching empathy, 24, 25, 26, 32; Teaching Excellence and Achievement Program (TEA), 32

global identification, 37

grades: academic vs. citizenship, 23; grading for mastery only, 16; importance to students and parents, 87–89; missing assignments, 21; negotiate grades, 68, 89; no-zero grading policy, 20–22; posting grades, 15–16, 19, 141

high expectations, 61

homework: assign or not, 19–20; growth mindset, 16; policy, 6, 139–140; value of, 16, 17

humility: intelligent humility, 26; power of, 66–67, 72

humor, 71–73

jumping to conclusions, 71

knowledge in your subject, 7

lesson planning: catching up, 139; over plan, 7; pacing, 12, 13; preparation, 9, 12, 140, 142; reuse, 9, 142

life-long learner, x, 15

mantra: personal, 141; school, 70, 138
medical emergency in classroom, 106
mentor program, 42–43
mentor teacher, 140

obedient children, 56
office hours, 9, 16, 68–69, 88, 140
oversharing vs. authentic, 59–61
own your career, ix

parenting, 56–57; blending into mainstream, 37; empower your children, 65–66; how to apologize, 66–67; step in for child, 67–68
part of the team at school, 41–43, 142
part of the team in retirement, 119–120; social isolation and loneliness, 119–120
part of the team outside of school, 83–84
patience at school, 71–74
patience in retirement, 125
patience outside of school, 105–107
peer observations. *See* reflection of others
perfect teacher, xii, 73
popular teacher, xii; being liked, 55, 64; cool teacher, 42, 53–54
positive at school, 45–50
positive in retirement, 121
positive outside of school, 85–86
post on social media, 103
prepared at school, 7–39
prepared in retirement, 115–118; five stages of retirement, 116–117
prepared outside of school, 81–82
present at school, 3–6
present in retirement, 111–113
present outside of school, 77–79
proactive at school, 51–70; proactive definition, 51
proactive in retirement, 123
proactive outside school, 87–103
professionalism: the 6 P's, xii, xv, 1

questions from University of Nevada (UNR) students, 138–143

racism. *See* global education
reflection of others, 10–11; effective classroom observation (eco), 43; self-reflection, 10, 11–13, 143
reteach a lesson, 5, 7, 71, 141
retirement, x; emotional plan, 116–117; financial plan, 117–118; legacy, 111, 117; on your terms, 111; purpose, 117, 120, 125; routines, 123; transition, 111–112, 123; when to tell everyone, 112
reviews: administrative, 142
role model, 35, 41, 45, 65
Rosemond, Dr. John. *See* parenting
rough day at school, 69–70, 86, 105
Rubinstein, Saul. *See* collaboration; future of education

school climate, 52–53; administrator's role, 53
self-advocacy, xii, 87–94; administrator demand, 90–91; administrator put down, 93; bullied, 94; death threat, 91; grade change demand, 89; overscheduled, 89–90; suspended, 91–93; teacher contract not followed, 94
self-care, 79–82, 85–94; mental health day, 78, 82; reenergize yourself, 85–86
setting boundaries: homework acceptance, 139–140; lunchtime, 68–69, 94; office hours, 68–69; professional vs. private life, 49, 68, 69, 82, 138–139; remote learning, 139; retirement, 112–113, 119; with stakeholders, xi
shaming, 12, 54, 78–79
singing with students, 73–74
special education students, 42, 95
stakeholders, xi
standards, 70, 143
student accountability, 5, 6, 21–22, 48
student civility, 22–23
student engagement, 46, 55–56; distracted, uninterested, 141; humor, 72; shy or quiet, 143
student feedback, 15–16, 17
student input, 11
student motivation, 7, 54
student teacher, 55, 107, 140
substitute teacher: establish a reputation, 55; lesson plans, 37–39

teacher leadership, x, 22, 127, 132–133, 137; leader vs. facilitator, 22, 51; negotiating with children, 56, 57, 68; qualities of a leader, 57–59
teacher rights, 94–103; Assembly Bill 521 (AB521), 94–96, 97; Empower Nevada Teachers (ENT), 97; job security and tenure, 101–103
teacher turnover, 131–132
teacher's union: Amanda Coffman, 89–90; join or not, 97–103; role of, 89–94, 100–101, 129; weaken, 98–100, 101, 129–130
teaching empathy. *See* global education
teaching with purpose, 22
technology: as a tool, 22; before technology, 29, 88; part of professional learning community (plc), 134; Power Points, 26, 30, 32; ready before lesson, 9; reflections, 12; substitute teacher, 38; technological literacy, 27
tests: policy, 19; retake, 67; standardized tests, 23, 99; student self-assess, 18–19; unannounced quizzes, 18; world language advanced placement (ap) exams, 30
tutor, 69

vandalism: classroom, 6; personal property, 89
vouchers, 98, 128

world language: immersion, 29–30; singing, 73–74

yoga, 77–78, 113, 125

ABOUT THE AUTHOR

Belle O'Neill retired in 2019 after thirty-two years as a public-school teacher in California and Nevada. She holds a bachelor's degree from Michigan State University in music education, a master's degree in music performance from the San Francisco Conservatory of Music, and a Spanish minor from the University of Nevada, Reno. She is a guest lecturer at the University of Nevada, Reno; Truckee Meadows Community College; Lake Tahoe Community College; and McQueen High School. Her topics include teacher rights, teacher credibility, communicating with parents, community and parental involvement at schools, and global education.

Belle was a 2016 Fulbright Fellow for Teachers for Global Classrooms to Colombia through the US Department of State. She also was a host teacher for many years for the Fulbright Teaching Excellence and Achievement Program. She organized and hosted two teachers and eight students from Colombia at a cultural exchange at McQueen High School in 2017 with the help of the Northern Nevada International Center of the University of Nevada, Reno. Belle currently lives in Reno, Nevada, with her family.